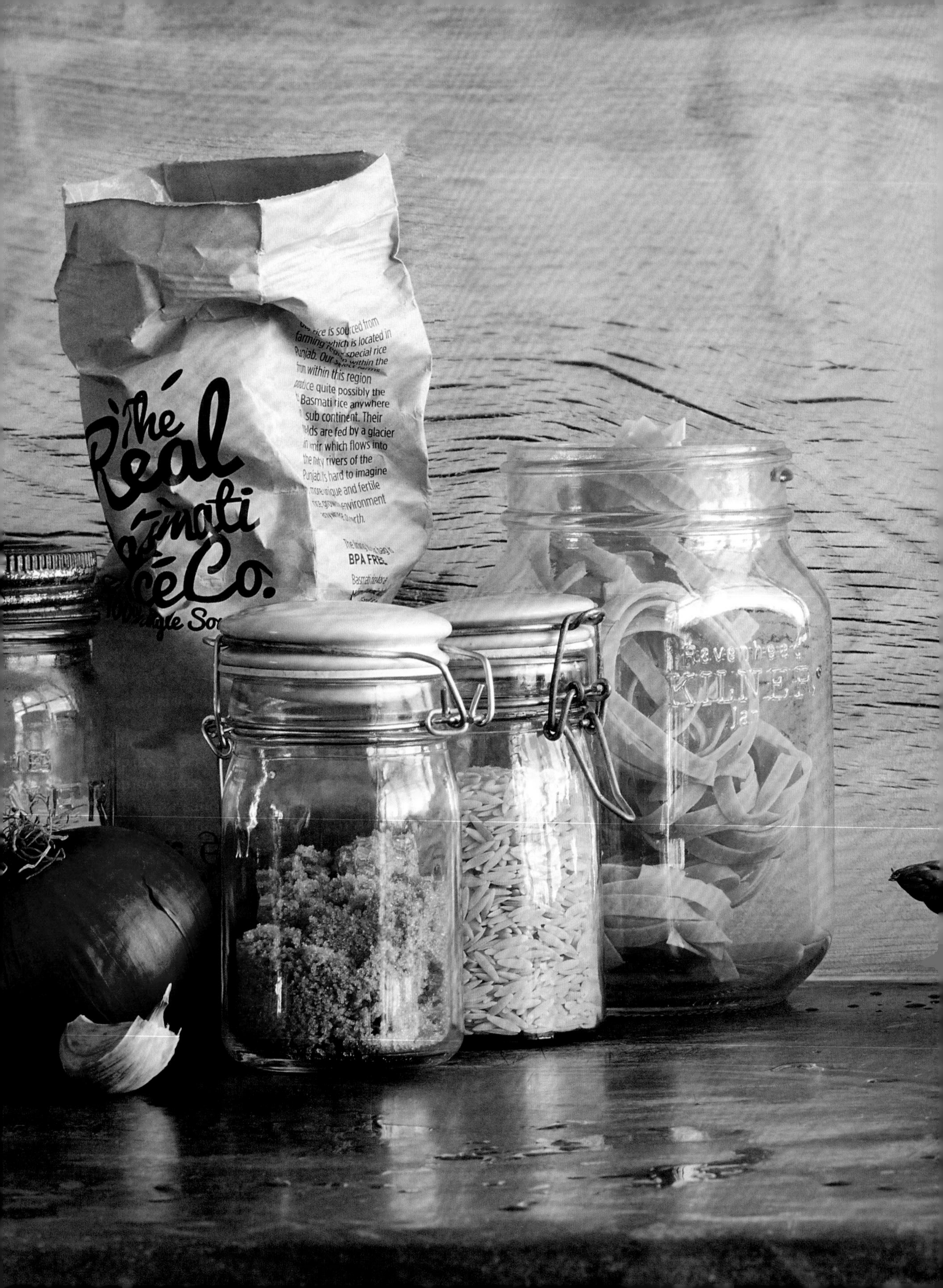
The Real
BPA FREE
KILNER

ANNABEL KARMEL'S
BUSY MUM'S
COOKBOOK

★

100 SIMPLE, DELICIOUS FAMILY RECIPES

EBURY PRESS

TO MY CHILDREN, NICHOLAS, LARA AND SCARLETT

10 9 8 7 6 5 4 3 2 1

Ebury Press, an imprint of Ebury Publishing,
20 Vauxhall Bridge Road,
London, SW1V 2SA

Ebury Press is part of the Penguin Random House group of companies
whose addresses can be found at global.penguinrandomhouse.com

Penguin
Random House
UK

First published by Ebury Press in 2015

www.eburypublishing.co.uk

A CIP catalogue record for this book is available
fom the British Library

Project editor: Laura Nickoll
Design and art direction: Smith & Gilmour
Photography: Susanna Blåvarg
Food stylist: Lucy O'Reilly
Prop stylist: Jenny Iggledon

ISBN: 9781785030888

Colour origination by Altaimage, London
Printed and bound in China by C&C Offset Printing Co., Ltd

Penguin Random House is committed to a sustainable future
for our business, our readers and our planet. This book is made from
Forest Stewardship Council® certified paper.

MIX
Paper from
responsible sources
FSC® C018179

CONTENTS

INTRODUCTION 8

20-MINUTE RECIPES 14
SIX INGREDIENTS 42
PREPARE AHEAD 74
LUNCHBOXES AND SNACKS 100
STORECUPBOARD 128
ENTERTAINING 148
SWEETS 180

INDEX 213
ABOUT THE AUTHOR 222
ACKNOWLEDGEMENTS 224

INTRODUCTION

I love nothing more than seeing dog-eared, tomato-stained copies of my cookbooks. It's incredibly satisfying to know that my recipes are relied upon time and time again, by families all over the world.

I'm also taken aback when new mothers bring me dishevelled first editions of my *Complete Baby & Toddler Meal Planner* to sign, telling me this was the 'bible' their mum used when they were a baby... and a toddler... and even in their teenage years. In fact, countless mums fondly relay their stories of rustling up my Chicken and Apple Balls for their grown-up dinner parties, or cooking my First Beef Bolognese for their husband's dinner because 'that's what he likes'. One mum recently told me that her daughter will only eat my Mini Cottage Pies from the *Complete Baby & Toddler Meal Planner*; her daughter is 20 and studying law at Exeter Iniversity, so she freezes and hand-delivers batches once a month.

If I'd known 25 years ago, when I was experimenting with different foods to get my baby son to eat, that I'd be inspiring generations of families with my recipes, I'd never have believed it.

Demystifying cooking for babies is one thing, but to then find that my recipes are being dished up for dinner parties, grown-up lunchboxes and student survival is a whole different ball game, and one that I wanted to address: delicious, simple recipes that will wow every family member, whatever their age.

Many of us stick with what we know and trust when it comes to cooking, especially as our lives are busier than ever. Yet the result is often a collection of six or seven failsafe recipes that families rely upon week in, week out.

I often wonder how many cookbooks are bought and displayed, but wind up collecting dust on the shelf. I'm sure I could set up a whole bookshop of beautifully pristine cookbooks I never use. I think many of us like the idea of taking on the Hestons and Ramsays of this world but, in reality, we feel safer and happier when we know what we're doing. Yet cooking something new doesn't have to be scary or time consuming. And to prove it, I've created a cookbook which uses a wide range of ingredients – some familiar and some you wouldn't necessarily think of using – to encourage variety and bags of flavour without the 'faff'.

You might have thought that duck, clams and quinoa were best left in the hands of the professionals, but I beg to differ. They are actually simple ingredients to find and cook with, without the need for flamboyant recipes or baffling cooking methods.

'Simplicity' is the common theme that runs through this book. Just like my cookbooks for babies and toddlers, every recipe is broken down into simple, manageable steps. And I've split them into categories that every busy family needs – 20-minute recipes, meals using no more than six ingredients, dishes you can prepare ahead, lunchboxes and snacks, storecupboard meals and ideas for entertaining.

In my book, you'll find simple classics which have stood the test of time, such as

Dover Sole with Herb Butter (see page 31) and Slow Roast Shoulder of Lamb with Potatoes and Leeks (see page 161). And then there are recipes inspired by my encounters with other culinary cultures. Wherever I might be in the world, I'll always duck out of a busy schedule to sample local dishes and scour food markets, soaking up the dazzling array of treats on offer. Take my Chicken and Vermicelli Thai Rice Wraps (see page 106); a healthy version of a spring roll, they originate from a backstreet market I stumbled upon in Hong Kong. Or my Sticky Coconut Chicken Thighs (see page 85), which were first served to me by a friend in Australia who invited me to her home for dinner.

Many of my recipes are inspired by the people around me. Take the Power Seed Bars (see page 109) – the brainchild of my South African friend Cheryl, who agreed to share her secret recipe after I devoured an entire batch during a coffee morning. I just had to include them in my book. I also worked with my good friend and talented chef Theo Randall on the children's menu for InterContinental Hotels & Resorts. With a world theme in mind, we would cook up our own ideas for each other to taste, and his Baked Tomato Risotto was a hands-down winner – so much so, I had to include it in my entertaining chapter (see page 150).

And then there are my home-grown recipes such as the Sweet Potato Curls (see page 61), which were the by-product of one shiny new spiraliser and one very bored daughter one Sunday afternoon. I'm not usually one for faddy gadgets, but I definitely believe the spiralizer should be a kitchen staple. You feed in raw veggies to produce perfectly formed curls and twirls which can be cooked in next to no time – and it makes food prep a lot more fun.

My children have always played a big part in my cooking, and what busy family life has taught me is that prepping ahead is the key to stress-free mealtimes. You never know what each day might throw at you, so having whole dishes or parts of one prepared in advance is a godsend. In fact, my 25-year-old son has recently benefitted from a few deliveries of my Mediterranean Oven-baked Chicken Drumsticks (see page 82) and Pasta Meatball Bake (see page 77). He's just moved into a new flat with a friend, so I've been stocking him up on frozen batches of his favourites. Nick is not a bad cook, but you never stop worrying that they're eating properly (especially Nick, as his fussiness got me into the business of food in the first place). Although apparently I've been catering for most of his friends too, as the requests are coming in thick and fast!

Honestly, my kitchen is like a café, with kids, friends and family (that includes my three dogs) buzzing in and out. But I wouldn't have it any other way.

Whilst my two girls haven't yet flown the nest, they both lead incredibly busy lives, dashing around like whirlwinds, so have been my inspiration for creating a range of 20-minute meals, such as the Beef with Oyster Sauce, Peppers and Broccoli (see page 40), to keep them (and their friends) going. They've always taken an interest in food – perhaps because they've been roped in as my chief taste testers since they were babies. They are without a doubt my biggest fans and my biggest critics, although I love the challenge of changing their minds when they tell me they don't like a particular food. Take Scarlett: she would always refuse to eat cauliflower, until I perfected my Roasted Cauliflower recipe (see page 63). Now she's a cauli-convert and we can't cook enough of the stuff.

For me, no family cookbook would be complete without simple ideas for lunchboxes and snacks. Packed lunches have always been a big deal in our household; the girls still leave the house for work armed with a stash of healthy snacks, and healthy lunchboxes to keep them going. Lara's favourite is my Italian Rice Salad (see page 110), a mix of chicken, rice, tomatoes, spring onion and toasted pine nuts with a dressing flavoured with freshly grated Parmesan. But it's not always easy to get into the habit of preparing lunches for school or work. And let's be honest, it can be all too easy to ditch the soggy ham sandwich in favour of the delights that the local deli or café has to offer, but nothing tastes as good as your own home-prepared food. Knowing what to make is the biggest challenge, so I've done all the hard work for you, with a series of really simple recipes that will have you and your family looking forward to lunch.

Finally, I believe in enjoying a little of what you fancy, and given my love

of baking, I've rounded up some of my favourite cookies, cakes and desserts. If I do say so myself, the Plum and Almond Cake (see page 199) should come with a warning, as it's so unbelievably delicious! A cross between a pudding and a cake, it will fill your home with beautiful aromas. And I never tire of jelly, particularly as it's so easy to make using leaf gelatine, which can be found in most supermarkets. My recipe with fresh raspberries and Prosecco (see page 206) is definitely one for that grown-up dinner party.

I hope my straight-talking recipes inspire you to change up your mealtimes and have a go at cooking with new ingredients. I want this book to become worn and well thumbed, with pages bookmarked, starred and folded. I want you to discover new dishes together as a family, and share the recipes with your friends. And don't forget to pass it down to your children and their children.

NOTE
All my recipes have been tested in a fan oven. If your oven is a conventional one, simply increase the temperature by 20°C.

MIRIN

A type of rice wine used in Japanese cooking and similar to sake, it gives an instant sweetness to sauces and dishes. I'm forever adding it to chicken and salmon.

CRÈME FRAICHE

Brings a distinctive flavour to sauces and is perfect with pasta and dishes such as my One-Pot Chicken (see page 165).

Ingredients
I can't live without

People are always fascinated to know what ingredients I keep to hand, so I thought I'd share with you those I regularly rely on to bring mealtimes to life in a hurry.

SWEET CHILLI SAUCE

Adds a touch of red chilli and garlic to dishes, plus a hint of sweetness. I like to add it to stir-fries and marinades. It also doubles up as tasty dip.

TOMATOES

Always have tomatoes to hand (fresh and canned) as they work in almost any dish, from soups, pasta sauces and curries to tagines and salads. especially love sweet cherry tomatoes.

SHALLOTS

They have a finer flavour than standard onion varieties, and add a unique, delicate, sweet flavour to stews and casseroles, as well as stir-fries, soups and sauces.

PARMESAN

Adding even the smallest amount of Parmesan cheese to recipes enhances the flavour. It's a good source of protein and calcium too.

DARK CHOCOLATE

Never deny yourself a little of what you fancy. My indulgence is a small square of organic extra-dark sea salt chocolate from Seed and Bean. (I tend to hide it where my family won't find it!)

FROZEN VEGETABLES

I don't like waste, so I'll always have frozen green veg to hand, such as peas, spinach and broccoli. Freezing is a great way to preserve important nutrients.

FRESH HERBS

Herbs can take a dish from good to great. Thyme adds incredible fragrant flavour to chicken and other meat.

WHOLE ROAST CHICKEN

So versatile that it's enjoyed by my whole family, including Bono, my American Cocker Spaniel, who has a taste for the finer things!

Chapter one
20-MINUTE RECIPES

CHICKEN AND VEGETABLE CHOWDER

PREP: 5 MINS
COOK: 15 MINS

15 g (½ oz) butter
1 onion, finely diced
100 g (4 oz) butternut squash, peeled, deseeded and diced
150 g (5 oz) floury potato, peeled and diced
2 x 198 g (7 oz) cans sweetcorn, drained
600 ml (1 pint) chicken stock
4 tbsp double cream
75 g (3 oz) cooked chicken, shredded
salt and black pepper

A delicious, warming blend of chicken and vegetables. I love the combination of potato, butternut squash and sweetcorn, but you could also use sweet potatoes if you don't have butternut squash to hand. Serve with crusty bread on the side.

STEP ONE Melt the butter in a saucepan, add the onion and sauté for 3–4 minutes until soft. Add the squash, potato and sweetcorn, then pour in the stock, cover and bring to the boil.

STEP TWO Simmer for 10 minutes, covered, until the potato and squash are tender.

STEP THREE Remove half of the soup from the saucepan and blend the rest with an electric hand blender, before returning the unblended soup to the pan. Add the double cream and shredded chicken, then simmer for 2 minutes. Season to taste before serving.

TIP
If you are short of time, buy pre-chopped vegetables, especially the ones that are cumbersome to chop, like butternut squash.

Makes 4 portions

ICEBERG AND CHERRY TOMATO SALAD WITH BLUE CHEESE DRESSING

PREP: 10 MINS

1 iceberg lettuce, cut
   into bite-sized pieces
200 g (7 oz) cherry tomatoes,
   halved

FOR THE DRESSING
1 tbsp Dijon mustard
1 tbsp white wine vinegar
6 tbsp olive oil
50 g (2 oz) Roquefort
   cheese, cubed
a pinch of caster sugar
squeeze of lemon juice

Crisp lettuce and blue cheese are a great combination, and the creamy dressing can be made in moments, by simply blitzing all the ingredients together.

STEP ONE Arrange the lettuce and tomatoes in a salad bowl. Measure all of the dressing ingredients into a bowl or jug, and blend until smooth using an electric hand blender.

STEP TWO Pour the dressing over the salad, toss and serve immediately.

Makes 4 portions

CHICKEN CHOW MEIN

A classic Chinese supper, drizzled in a tangy sauce. Packed full of fresh vegetables, with added chilli for a hit of spice, this is convenience food at its best.

PREP: 8 MINS
COOK: 10 MINS

125 g (4½ oz) medium
   egg noodles
2 tbsp sunflower oil
2 skinless chicken breasts,
   cut into thin strips
2 carrots, thinly sliced
   lengthways or cut
   into matchsticks
100 g (4 oz) button
   mushrooms, sliced
200 g (7 oz) sugar snap peas,
   thickly sliced lengthways
2 pak choi, sliced widthways
½ red chilli, deseeded
   and diced
salt and black pepper

FOR THE SAUCE
2 tbsp dry sherry
2 tbsp soy sauce
2 tbsp oyster sauce
1 tbsp caster sugar
1 tbsp sesame oil
1 tbsp cornflour
1 garlic clove, crushed

STEP ONE Cook the noodles in lightly salted boiling water according to the packet instructions, until soft. Drain, refresh under cold running water, and set aside.

STEP TWO Meanwhile, heat half the oil in a wok or frying pan. Season the chicken strips and fry over a high heat until brown and cooked through. Remove from the wok and set aside.

STEP THREE Add the remaining oil to the wok and return to the heat. Add the vegetables and chilli and stir-fry for 3 minutes over a high heat. Add the cooked noodles and chicken. Mix the ingredients for the sauce together in a bowl. Add the sauce to the wok and toss over a high heat. Remove from the heat and serve immediately.

Makes 4 portions

PUY LENTILS WITH MUSHROOMS AND SPINACH

PREP: 8 MINS
COOK: 12 MINS

2 tbsp olive oil
1 onion, finely chopped
2 garlic cloves, crushed
250 g (9 oz) button
   mushrooms, sliced
250 g (9 oz) packet cooked
   Puy lentils
200 g (7 oz) spinach leaves
100 ml (3½ fl oz) double cream
25 g (1 oz) Parmesan
   cheese, grated
squeeze of lemon juice
salt and black pepper

Puy lentils are considered by many to be the finest type of lentils, and I like to save time by buying the pre-cooked variety. This combination of mushrooms and spinach with a creamy Parmesan cheese sauce is the perfect way to serve them.

STEP ONE Heat the olive oil in a frying pan over a medium heat and sauté the onion for 5 minutes, until soft. Add the button mushrooms and fry for 4–5 minutes, until golden, then add the garlic and fry for a further minute.

STEP TWO Increase the heat and add the lentils and spinach. Fry for 2 minutes, stirring, then remove the pan from the heat and add the double cream, grated Parmesan and lemon juice. Stir until the cheese has melted. Season to taste and serve.

CHICKEN BOLOGNESE WITH PENNE

PREP: 5 MINS
COOK: 15 MINS

1 tbsp olive oil
2 onions, finely chopped
½ red chilli, deseeded
   and finely diced
2 garlic cloves, crushed
350 g (12 oz) minced chicken
100 g (4 oz) button
   mushrooms, sliced
400 g (14 oz) can cream
   of tomato soup
400 g (14 oz) can chopped
   tomatoes
2 tbsp sundried tomato paste
1 tbsp chopped fresh
   thyme leaves
250 g (9 oz) penne
salt and black pepper

Swap beef mince for chicken mince in this twist on a traditional family favourite. Serve with pasta and a slice of garlic bread.

STEP ONE Heat the olive oil in a frying pan over a medium heat. Add the onion, chilli and garlic and sauté for 2–3 minutes, until soft. Add the mince and fry until it starts to brown, breaking up any lumps with a wooden spoon. Add the mushrooms and fry for 3 minutes, then add the soup, chopped tomatoes, tomato paste and thyme leaves.

STEP TWO Season and bring to the boil, then simmer uncovered for 10 minutes, until the sauce has reduced and the vegetables are tender.

STEP THREE Meanwhile, cook the pasta in a large saucepan of lightly salted boiling water according to the packet instructions. Drain and toss with the sauce.

Makes 4 portions

FETTUCCINE WITH CHICKEN AND SPINACH

PREP: 10 MINS
COOK: 10 MINS

2 tbsp olive oil
1 onion, chopped
2 garlic cloves, crushed
2 skinless chicken breasts,
    sliced into strips
150 ml (¼ pint) Marsala wine
200 g (7 oz) crème fraîche
150 g (5 oz) baby spinach
    leaves
50 g (2 oz) Parmesan cheese,
    grated
250 g (9 oz) fettuccine
salt and black pepper

Get everyone heading to the dinner table in a hurry with this luxurious, creamy pasta dish. Adding spinach and Parmesan cheese really boosts the colour and taste.

STEP ONE Heat the olive oil in a frying pan over a medium heat. Add the onion and garlic and sauté for 2–3 minutes, until soft. Add the chicken strips and fry until browned, then pour in the marsala and bring up to the boil. Add the crème fraîche, simmer for a minute, then add the spinach and Parmesan cheese.

STEP TWO Meanwhile, cook the pasta in a large saucepan of lightly salted boiling water according to the packet instructions. Drain, and add the pasta to the sauce. Toss together and season to taste before serving.

DUCK STIR-FRY WITH PLUM SAUCE

PREP: 8 MINS
COOK: 12 MINS

2 x 150 g (5 oz) skinless duck
   breasts, cut into strips
4 tbsp plum sauce
2 tbsp sunflower oil
1 yellow pepper, deseeded
   and sliced
2 shallots, sliced
200 g (7 oz) button
   mushrooms, sliced
250 g (9 oz) sugar snap peas
2 pak choi, leaves separated
2 tbsp soy sauce
1 tsp grated fresh root ginger
1 tsp cornflour
salt and black pepper

Give your stir-fry a sweet and sour edge with a dash of plum sauce, soy sauce and ginger. The oriental flavours are a perfect match for duck breast. Serve with rice or stir-fried vegetables.

STEP ONE Season the duck strips and coat them in 2 tablespoons of the plum sauce. Heat the sunflower oil in a wok or frying pan until hot and add the duck strips. Fry for 8–10 minutes until golden, then remove and set aside. Add the yellow pepper, shallot, mushrooms, sugar snap peas and pak choi leaves to the wok over a high heat and stir-fry for a few minutes.

STEP TWO Mix together the remaining plum sauce, soy sauce, ginger and cornflour. Pour the mixture into the wok and add the cooked duck. Toss over the heat for a minute or two until heated through and serve immediately.

TIP
Use a teaspoon to peel the skin off fresh root ginger.

CHICKEN IN BARBECUE SAUCE

PREP: 5 MINS
COOK: 15 MINS

1 tbsp sunflower oil
1 onion, chopped
1 garlic clove, finely chopped
1 carrot, thinly sliced
300 ml (½ pint) chicken stock
3 tbsp tomato ketchup
2 tbsp soy sauce
2 tsp soft brown sugar
2 tsp Worcestershire sauce
1 tsp balsamic vinegar
2 tbsp cornflour
450 g (1 lb) skinless chicken
    breasts, cut into strips
2 tsp runny honey
salt and black pepper

This dish is always popular with children. Tossing the chicken in a little honey before stir-frying makes it irresistibly moreish. Serve with fluffy basmati rice.

STEP ONE Heat the sunflower oil in a saucepan over a medium heat, add the onion and sauté for 3 minutes, until soft. Meanwhile, steam or cook the sliced carrot in boiling water for 5 minutes, then drain. Add the garlic to the onion and fry for 30 seconds.

STEP TWO Add the stock, ketchup, soy sauce, sugar, Worcestershire sauce and balsamic vinegar to the onion and garlic. Mix the cornflour with 2 tablespoons of cold water until smooth, then add to the sauce and stir for a minute until thickened.

STEP THREE Season the chicken and toss with the honey. Fry the chicken in a separate frying pan until browned, then add the chicken to the sauce with the carrots and simmer for 5 minutes. Season to taste.

Makes 4 portions

PENNE WITH ROASTED CHERRY TOMATOES AND PESTO

PREP: 6 MINS
COOK: 10 MINS

300 g (11 oz) small cherry
    or plum tomatoes
1 tbsp balsamic vinegar
1 tbsp olive oil
1 garlic clove, crushed
275 g (10 oz) penne
5 tbsp fresh green pesto
125 g (4½ oz) mini
    mozzarella balls
4 tbsp chopped fresh
    basil leaves
salt and black pepper

If you're in need of a speedy meal, give this recipe a go; tomato and pesto is always a crowd-pleasing combination.

STEP ONE Preheat the oven to 200°C/400°F/Gas 6.

STEP TWO Put the tomatoes, balsamic vinegar, olive oil and garlic in a small roasting tin. Roast in the oven for 5 minutes, then season to taste.

STEP THREE Meanwhile, cook the penne in a large saucepan of lightly salted boiling water according to the packet instructions, then drain.

STEP FOUR Add the pesto to the pasta and toss together with the roasted tomatoes and their juices, the mozzarella and basil. Season and serve immediately.

PAPPARDELLE WITH DOLCELATTE, SPINACH AND TOMATO

PREP: 6 MINS
COOK: 10 MINS

300 g (11 oz) pappardelle
150 g (5 oz) baby spinach
   leaves, chopped
a little oil, for frying
1 garlic clove, crushed
200 g (7 oz) cherry tomatoes,
   halved, or quartered if large
100 ml (3½ fl oz) double cream
150 g (5 oz) Dolcelatte
   cheese, or other soft
   blue cheese, cubed
juice of ½ lemon
salt and black pepper

Rich and creamy, this simple and comforting pasta dish is lifted with the addition of spinach and tomatoes, which balance out the saltiness of the blue cheese.

STEP ONE Cook the pasta in a large saucepan of lightly salted boiling water according to the packet instructions, adding the spinach just before draining.

STEP TWO Meanwhile, heat a little oil in a frying pan over a low heat, add the garlic and tomatoes and fry for 2–3 minutes to soften, then add the cream and cheese, stirring until the cheese has melted. Add the cooked pasta, spinach and lemon juice.

STEP THREE Toss everything together over the heat for a minute or two, then season to taste and serve.

*Makes 4 portions
(freezer friendly)*

TOMATO AND MASCARPONE SAUCE

**PREP: 6 MINS
COOK: 14 MINS**

1 tbsp olive oil
1 onion, chopped
1 garlic clove, crushed
400 g (14 oz) can
   chopped tomatoes
½ tsp mixed dried herbs
1 tbsp sundried tomato paste
1 tsp soft light brown sugar
2 tbsp chopped fresh
   basil leaves
2 tbsp mascarpone
salt and black pepper

This simple, popular sauce is a real winner, and is endlessly versatile: mix in cooked prawns, perhaps, or add diced ham or cooked chicken. Serve with pasta.

STEP ONE Heat the olive oil in a saucepan, add the onion and garlic and sauté for 2–3 minutes, until soft. Add the tomatoes, herbs, sundried tomato paste and brown sugar.

STEP TWO Bring to the boil, cover and simmer for 10 minutes. Add the basil and mascarpone, then blend until smooth using an electric hand blender. Season to taste.

TIP
It's easy to dry leftover fresh herbs at home. Simply bunch the herbs together, tie with string and hang them upside down. When completely dry, store in a jar.

DOVER SOLE WITH HERB BUTTER

PREP: 5 MINS
COOK: 11–14 MINS

2 medium Dover sole, skin
    removed on both sides
    and heads removed
50 g (2 oz) butter, softened
1 tbsp chopped fresh
    parsley leaves
1 tbsp snipped chives
squeeze of lemon juice
salt and black pepper

Herb butters go so well with fish. You could swap the chives for finely chopped dill in this herb butter if you liked, or use an alternative flat fish such as lemon sole or turbot.

STEP ONE Preheat the oven to 200°C/400°F/Gas 6 and line a large baking sheet with non-stick baking paper.

STEP TWO Put the fish on a chopping board and season both sides. Beat the butter and herbs together and spread the herb butter over one side of each of the fish.

STEP THREE Heat a large frying pan until hot. Add one fish, butter-side down, and fry for 3–4 minutes until lightly golden. Carefully flip the fish onto the prepared baking sheet, browned side up. Repeat with the second fish. Bake the fish for 8–10 minutes, until golden and the flesh is just coming away from the bone.

STEP FOUR Transfer to a plate, squeeze over a little lemon juice and pour over the buttery juices from the baking sheet. Serve with new potatoes and spinach.

TIP
Freeze herb butter and you'll always have some to hand: after beating the butter and parsley together, scoop it onto a piece of clingfilm and roll it into a sausage. Freeze, then slice off discs of herb butter when you need them.

Makes 2–3 portions (freezer friendly)

COD IN CHEESY SAUCE

PREP: 6 MINS
COOK: 14 MINS

25 g (1 oz) butter
1 onion, finely chopped
2 level tbsp plain flour
2 tsp rice wine vinegar
300 ml (½ pint) warm
  whole milk
25 g (1 oz) Parmesan
  cheese, grated
250 g (9 oz) skinless cod loin,
  cut into 3 cm (1 in) chunks
2 tbsp snipped chives
salt and black pepper

Creamy cheese sauce and flaky fish go hand in hand and are a classic combination. This light and tasty dish is best served with steamed vegetables and mashed potato or rice.

STEP ONE To make the sauce, melt the butter in a saucepan over a medium heat, then add the onion and sauté for 5 minutes until soft. Stir in the flour, add the vinegar, cook for a minute, then gradually stir in the milk. Once all the milk has been incorporated, bring the sauce to the boil, and cook, stirring, until thickened. Add the Parmesan cheese, mixing to melt, then season to taste and gently stir in the chunks of cod.

STEP TWO Simmer gently for 3–4 minutes, until the fish is cooked. Add the chives and serve.

TIP
To prevent lumps in your cheese sauce, warm the milk before stirring it into the flour and butter.

PRAWNS IN A LIGHT CURRIED SAUCE

PREP: 6 MINS
COOK: 14 MINS

2 tbsp olive oil
1 onion, finely chopped
2½ tsp korma curry paste
1 tsp tomato purée
3 tbsp brandy
250 g (9 oz) full-fat
    crème fraîche
1 tsp mango chutney
squeeze of lemon juice
a knob of butter
350 g (12 oz) raw king
    prawns, peeled but tail
    and shell left on
salt and black pepper

This gentle curry offers maximum flavour from the korma paste, brandy, mango chutney and crème fraîche, and is super-quick to make.

STEP ONE To make the sauce, heat 1 tablespoon of the olive oil in a saucepan over a medium heat, add the onion and sauté for 5 minutes until soft. Add the curry paste and tomato purée, then add the brandy. Let the sauce bubble away for a few seconds before adding the crème fraîche, mango chutney and lemon juice. Bring to the boil, then remove from the heat and blend until smooth using an electric hand blender.

STEP TWO Heat a large frying pan until very hot, then add the remaining oil and the butter. Once the butter is foaming, add the prawns and fry until pink and starting to brown. Add the sauce and bring to the boil. Season to taste, and add a little water if the sauce is too thick. Serve with basmati rice.

PREP: 15 MINS
COOK: 5 MINS

1 tsp grated fresh root ginger
1 bunch spring onions,
    chopped
200 g (7 oz) raw, peeled
    king prawns
50 g (2 oz) Japanese
    panko breadcrumbs
1 tsp soy sauce
1 tsp sesame oil
1 tsp sweet chilli sauce
sunflower oil, for frying
25 g (1 oz) sesame seeds,
    toasted (see tip on page 104)
salt and black pepper
lime wedges, to serve

SESAME PRAWN BALLS

These sesame prawn balls make a great starter
or dinner-party canapé. Serve with a lime or sweet
chilli dipping sauce, for added zing.

STEP ONE Place the ginger and spring onions in the
bowl of a food processor. Whizz until roughly chopped,
then add the prawns, panko breadcrumbs, soy sauce,
sesame oil and sweet chilli sauce. Whizz again, until
finely chopped and combined.

STEP TWO Season the mixture and shape into 20 balls.

STEP THREE Heat a little sunflower oil in a frying pan.
Fry the balls for about 5 minutes, until golden and
cooked through. Once cooked, put the toasted sesame
seeds on a plate and roll each ball in the seeds,
transferring them to a plate covered with kitchen
paper to drain.

TROUT WITH ALMONDS

PREP: 5 MINS
COOK: 15 MINS

2 fresh rainbow trout,
  scaled, gutted, cleaned
  and oven ready (your
  fishmonger could do this)
1 bunch thyme sprigs
50 g (2 oz) butter
2 tbsp olive oil
2 tbsp snipped chives
squeeze of lemon juice
100 g (4 oz) flaked almonds,
  toasted (see tip on page 104)
salt and black pepper
lemon wedges, to serve

The flesh of rainbow trout can be white or pink, and has a delicate, almost nutty flavour that works perfectly with toasted almonds.

STEP ONE Preheat the oven to 200°C/400°F/Gas 6.

STEP TWO Season the fish inside and out, and stuff the cavities with the thyme.

STEP THREE Melt half the butter with the olive oil in a large ovenproof frying pan over a medium heat. When the butter is sizzling, fry both the trout on one side for about 4 minutes until golden. Turn over the fish and place the pan in the oven.

STEP FOUR Bake for 8–10 minutes, until the flesh is just coming away from the bone. When cooked through, transfer to a plate.

STEP FIVE Add the remaining butter to the pan on the hob. Add the chives and a squeeze of lemon juice. Spoon over the fish and top with toasted flaked almonds. Serve with new potatoes and a green salad on the side.

Makes 4 baguettes

STEAK BAGUETTES WITH TOMATO AND ONION RELISH

PREP: 10 MINS
COOK: 5 MINS

1 long, thin baguette
a little mayonnaise
2 x 200 g (7 oz) thin
    sirloin steaks
salt and black pepper
rocket leaves, to serve

FOR THE RELISH
½ small red onion,
    finely sliced
100 g (4 oz) cherry
    tomatoes, quartered
2 tsp balsamic vinegar
2 tbsp olive oil

Minute-steak baguettes take hardly any time to make, and they taste great. Go that extra mile and serve them with homemade tomato and onion relish.

STEP ONE Cut the baguette into 4 pieces and slice each piece in half horizontally. Spread a little mayonnaise over one side of each half.

STEP TWO Season the steaks, then heat a frying pan until hot. Fry the steaks for 2½ minutes on each side until cooked but still pink in the middle. Set aside on a plate and leave to rest.

STEP THREE Place the onion slices in a heatproof bowl, pour over boiling water to cover, leave for 5 minutes, then strain, cool under cold running water and pat dry. To make the relish, mix together the soaked onion, tomatoes, balsamic vinegar and oil.

STEP FOUR Cut each steak into thin slices and divide the slices between each baguette. Top with the relish and rocket leaves and serve immediately.

BEEF WITH OYSTER SAUCE, PEPPERS AND BROCCOLI

PREP: 10 MINS
COOK: 10 MINS

350 g (12 oz) beef fillet or
   sirloin steak, cut into
   medium strips
3 tbsp sunflower oil
150 g (5 oz) Tenderstem
   broccoli
1 yellow and 1 red pepper,
   deseeded and thinly sliced
1 red onion, thinly sliced
salt and black pepper

FOR THE SAUCE
3 tbsp soy sauce
2 tbsp runny honey
4 tbsp oyster sauce
1 garlic clove, crushed

This is a quick-as-a-flash supper, and tossing the beef in honey and soy sauce before stir-frying gives it a wonderful sweet-savoury Asian flavour.

STEP ONE Put the beef strips into a bowl and coat with 1 tablespoon of the soy sauce and 1 tablespoon of the honey. Toss together and season.

STEP TWO Mix the remaining sauce ingredients together.

STEP THREE Heat 2 tablespoons of the sunflower oil in a wok or frying pan until hot and stir-fry the beef over a high heat for about 2 minutes, until browned, then set aside.

STEP FOUR Heat the remaining tablespoon of oil in the wok, add the broccoli and stir-fry for 2 minutes, then add the peppers and onion and stir-fry for a further 2 minutes. Add the sauce ingredients and simmer for 1 minute, then add the beef and toss together until the broccoli is just cooked. Serve immediately with rice.

TIP
To save time, heat your pan while you're preparing the ingredients. It's much better to start with a hot pan on the stove and then add the oil.

Chapter two
SIX INGREDIENTS

Makes 4 portions

MUSHROOM AND BROCCOLI PASTA

PREP: 10 MINS
COOK: 15 MINS

250 g (9 oz) fusilli
   (or similar pasta shape)
100 g (4 oz) broccoli florets
2 tbsp olive oil
350 g (12 oz) brown
   mushrooms, sliced
250 g (9 oz) full-fat
   crème fraîche
100 ml (3½ fl oz)
   vegetable stock
50 g (2 oz) Parmesan
   cheese, grated
salt and black pepper

Adding crème fraîche and Parmesan cheese to cooked vegetables is a great way to make a speedy pasta sauce. Serve with a leaf salad and cherry tomatoes.

STEP ONE Cook the pasta in a large saucepan of lightly salted boiling water according to the packet instructions. Four minutes before the end of the cooking time, add the broccoli florets. Drain.

STEP TWO Heat the olive oil in a frying pan. Add the mushrooms and fry over a high heat for 3 minutes until just cooked and slightly golden. Add the crème fraîche and stock to the pan, heat through, then add the cooked pasta and broccoli, and season.

STEP THREE Remove from the heat and sprinkle with the Parmesan. Toss together before serving.

TIP
Leave your Parmesan cheese out of the fridge for a while before you need to use it. It's much easier to grate at room temperature.

THREE-CHEESE RIGATONI

PREP: 10 MINS
COOK: 15 MINS

300 g (11 oz) rigatoni
250 g (9 oz) full-fat
   crème fraîche
30 g (1¼ oz) Parmesan
   cheese, grated
50 g (2 oz) Cheddar
   cheese, grated
50 g (2 oz) Roquefort or
   other blue cheese, cubed
3 tbsp snipped chives
salt and black pepper

I like blue cheese, but it's not popular with everyone so you could substitute Gruyère, if you prefer. Serve this rich dish with a fresh green salad, for contrast.

STEP ONE Cook the pasta in a large saucepan of lightly salted boiling water according to the packet instructions, then drain.

STEP TWO Heat the crème fraîche in a large frying pan over a medium heat. Add the cooked pasta and toss over the heat. Add the cheeses and season. Remove from the heat, and stir until melted, then add the snipped chives.

TIP
Use kitchen scissors to snip delicate herbs like chives.

Makes 4 portions

BACON AND PEA RISOTTO

PREP: 12 MINS
COOK: 25–30 MINS

1 litre (1¾ pints)
    chicken stock
1 tbsp olive oil
150 g (5 oz) smoked
    bacon lardons
1 large onion, chopped
275 g (10 oz) risotto rice
100 g (4 oz) frozen peas
50 g (2 oz) Parmesan
    cheese, grated
salt and black pepper

This is a great midweek dinner. Using smoked bacon lardons brings a lovely rich, woody flavour to the dish.

STEP ONE Bring the stock to the boil in a saucepan and leave to simmer.

STEP TWO Heat the olive oil in a saucepan over a medium heat, add the bacon and fry until browned. Remove the bacon with a slotted spoon, add the onions and fry for 5 minutes, until softened. Add the risotto rice and stir until well coated, then return the bacon to the pan.

STEP THREE Add a ladleful of hot stock to the rice, stirring until all of the stock has been absorbed. Repeat, adding the stock a ladleful at a time, stirring continuously, until all the stock has been incorporated, and the rice is cooked (this will take about 20 minutes).

STEP FOUR Add the peas and stir over the heat until they have defrosted. Stir through the Parmesan, season to taste, and serve at once.

Makes 1 portion

SCRAMBLED EGGS WITH TOMATO AND ONION

PREP: 5 MINUTES
COOK: 10 MINUTES

15 g (½ oz) butter
1 small onion, finely chopped
1 small garlic clove,
    finely chopped
100 g (4 oz) tomatoes
    (salad or cherry), sliced
2 eggs, lightly beaten
1 tsp soy sauce
salt and black pepper

This is my children's favourite breakfast recipe: a sure-fire hit for all the family, in fact, and endlessly versatile. Just multiply the ingredients according to how many mouths you're feeding.

STEP ONE Melt the butter in a small non-stick frying pan over a medium heat and sauté the onion and garlic for 3 minutes, stirring. Add the sliced tomatoes and cook for a further 5 minutes, or until they start to break down.

STEP TWO Beat the eggs together with the soy sauce and a little salt and pepper. Add the beaten egg mixture to the tomato and onion and cook for a couple of minutes, stirring, or until the eggs are just set. Serve immediately.

TIP
Try adding a generous pinch of chicken stock powder or bouillon when you beat the eggs, to give the dish extra oomph.

HERB-CRUSTED SALMON

PREP: 10 MINS
COOK: 15 MINS

4 x 150 g (5 oz) skinless
  salmon fillets
25 g (1 oz) unsalted
  butter, softened
2 tbsp chopped fresh dill
4 tbsp Japanese panko
  breadcrumbs
½ tsp grated lemon zest
salt and black pepper

Japanese panko breadcrumbs are lighter than ordinary breadcrumbs. Mixed with fresh dill and grated lemon zest they make a tasty topping, and if you like you could add some chives. Avoid overcooking the fish; I think salmon is best eaten when it's still pink in the middle. Griddled Courgettes with Balsamic Glaze (see page 70) make a perfect accompaniment to this dish.

STEP ONE Preheat the oven to 180°C/350°F/Gas 4 and line a baking tray with non-stick baking paper.

STEP TWO Arrange the salmon fillets on the baking sheet and season. Mix the butter and dill together, then spread the herb butter over one side of each fillet. Press the breadcrumbs onto the butter, and sprinkle over the lemon zest.

STEP THREE Bake for 12–15 minutes, or until the salmon is cooked but still pink in the middle, and the crust is lightly golden and crisp.

Makes 4 portions

ROASTED CHICKEN AND TARRAGON PAPPARDELLE

PREP: 10 MINS
COOK: 15 MINS

250 g (9 oz) pappardelle
300 ml (½ pint) chicken stock
200 g (7 oz) full-fat
   crème fraîche
2 tbsp chopped fresh tarragon
   leaves, plus extra whole
   leaves to serve
2 x 300 g (11 oz) roasted
   skinless chicken breasts,
   sliced into strips
30 g (1¼ oz) Parmesan
   cheese, grated
salt and black pepper

A very simple but tasty pasta dish. The reduced, strong chicken stock in the sauce gives the pasta a wonderful depth of flavour. Serve with a tomato, avocado and mozzarella salad with a fresh basil garnish.

STEP ONE Cook the pasta in a saucepan of lightly salted boiling water according to the packet instructions, then drain.

STEP TWO Meanwhile, put the chicken stock in a large, deep frying pan. Reduce the stock over a high heat until you have about 200 ml (7 fl oz).

STEP THREE Add the crème fraîche to the stock and bring back up to the boil. Add the chopped tarragon and the chicken and simmer for 3–4 minutes. Add the cooked pasta to the sauce with the Parmesan. Season, toss together and serve, scattered with the whole tarragon leaves.

Makes 6 portions

HONEY-GLAZED CHICKEN WITH LEMON AND THYME

PREP: 10 MINS
COOK: 1 HOUR

1.6–1.8 kg (3½–4 lb) chicken
2 tbsp olive oil
grated zest and juice
  of 1 small lemon
1 garlic clove, crushed
2 tbsp runny honey
1 tbsp chopped fresh
  thyme leaves
salt and black pepper

This easy, classic Sunday lunch dish is made even more mouthwatering with the sweet and summery combination of lemon, honey and thyme. Serve with roast potatoes and seasonal vegetables.

STEP ONE Preheat the oven to 200°C/400°F/Gas 6.

STEP TWO Season the chicken and place it in a roasting tin. Drizzle over the olive oil. Roast for 45 minutes, until lightly golden and nearly cooked through.

STEP THREE Meanwhile, mix together the lemon juice and zest, garlic, honey and thyme. Remove the chicken from the oven, pour over the lemon and thyme mixture, then return to the oven for a further 15–20 minutes, until the chicken is cooked through and golden brown.

STEP FOUR If you would like gravy, add 300 ml (½ pint) chicken stock to the roasting tray, after you've removed the cooked chicken. Place over a high heat. Bring to the boil to deglaze. Thicken with 2 tablespoons of cornflour if it is a little thin.

TIP
If you have leftover cut lemons, squeeze out the juice and freeze it in ice cube trays.

ROASTED NEW POTATOES WITH ROSEMARY

PREP: 5 MINS
COOK: 30-45 MINS

1 kg (2¼ lb) baby new potatoes, scrubbed
3 tbsp olive oil
1 tbsp chopped fresh rosemary leaves
1 garlic clove, sliced
1 tsp sea salt
black pepper, to taste

Crisp up your new potatoes with a generous drizzle of olive oil and sea salt. The addition of rosemary gives them a wonderful aromatic flavour. Serve these as an accompaniment to roast chicken – they pair perfectly with my Mediterranean Oven-baked Chicken Drumsticks (see page 82) or Honey-glazed Chicken with Lemon and Thyme (see opposite).

STEP ONE Preheat the oven to 200°C/400°F/Gas 6.

STEP TWO Put all of the ingredients into a shallow roasting tin. Toss together, and roast for 30–45 minutes until golden brown and crisp.

TIP
When using herbs with woody stems like rosemary, sage and thyme, the easiest and quickest way to remove the leaves is to hold the top of the stem in one hand and strip the leaves down in the opposite direction from which they grow with the other hand.

Makes 14 goujons

CHICKEN GOUJONS WRAPPED IN PARMA HAM

PREP: 15 MINS
COOK: 10 MINS

2 large skinless
 chicken breasts
6 slices Parma ham
2 tsp runny honey
salt and black pepper

FOR THE SAUCE
200 g (7 oz) crème fraîche
2 tbsp fresh green pesto
squeeze of lemon juice

Add an extra flavour dimension to chicken goujons by wrapping them in Parma ham. They taste even better dunked into a creamy, zesty sauce, which you can dish up hot or cold. Serve with baked potato or sweet potato wedges.

STEP ONE Preheat the oven to 200°C/400°F/Gas 6 and grease a baking tin.

STEP TWO Place the chicken breasts on a board. Cover them with clingfilm, then bash them with a rolling pin until they are slightly thinner. Remove the clingfilm and slice each breast into 7 goujon-shaped strips.

STEP THREE Cut each slice of Parma ham in half. Wrap each goujon in a piece of parma ham, then place on the prepared baking tray. Drizzle over the honey, then roast for 10 minutes, until cooked through and crisp.

STEP FOUR Mix together the crème fraîche, pesto and lemon juice and season. Serve hot (heated through in a small saucepan) or cold with the crisp goujons.

Makes 4 portions

LINGUINE WITH HAM

PREP: 10 MINS
COOK: 12 MINS

275 g (10 oz) linguine
1 tbsp olive oil
1 bunch spring onions,
    thinly sliced
125 g (4½ oz) thickly sliced
    smoked ham, diced
50 g (2 oz) butter
2 tomatoes, deseeded and diced
75g (3 oz) Parmesan cheese,
    grated
salt and black pepper

This heart-warming, creamy dish is a perfect for a mid-week dinner. Make sure to add a generous scattering of grated Parmesan cheese to give it that delicious, piquant taste. Serve with a fresh green salad on the side.

STEP ONE Cook the linguine in a large saucepan of lightly salted boiling water according to the packet instructions, retaining 75 ml (3 fl oz) of the cooking water before draining.

STEP TWO Heat the olive oil in a large frying pan over a medium heat. Add the spring onions and ham and fry gently for 2–3 minutes, then add the butter and toss with the spring onions and ham until melted. Add the reserved cooking water, cooked linguine, diced tomatoes and 50 g (2 oz) of the Parmesan.

STEP THREE Toss together over a medium heat until the pasta is coated in the sauce, season well, then spoon into a serving dish and scatter with the remaining Parmesan.

Makes 6 portions

TOAD IN THE HOLE

PREP: 8 MINS
COOK: 45 MINS

1 tbsp olive oil
12 thin sausages, such
  as chipolatas
100 g (4 oz) plain flour
3 medium eggs
200 ml (7 fl oz) whole milk
salt and black pepper

Choose your favourite sausages and cook them in this Yorkshire pudding batter. You can serve this classic crowd-pleaser with the gravy from the Minced Beef Croquettes (see page 91), and steamed vegetables.

STEP ONE Preheat the oven to 200°C/400°F/Gas 6 and grease a roasting tin with the olive oil.

STEP TWO Arrange the sausages in the base of the greased tin and roast for 15 minutes, then turn the sausages so the browned sides are facing up.

STEP THREE Place the flour in a bowl, add the eggs and whisk until smooth. Gradually whisk in the milk until you have a smooth batter, then season.

STEP FOUR Take the roasting tin out of the oven and pour the batter over the sausages. Return to the oven for another 30 minutes, until the batter is well risen and golden brown.

SWEET POTATO CURLS

PREP: 2 MINS
COOK: 20 MINS

1 large sweet potato, peeled
4 tbsp mild olive oil
salt and black pepper

If you have never used a spiraliser, it really is the most fantastic kitchen gadget. It also adds oodles of child appeal to everyday vegetables.

STEP ONE Preheat the oven to 200°C/400°F/Gas 6 and line two baking sheets with non-stick baking paper.

STEP TWO Put the sweet potato through a spiraliser to make long, spaghetti-like strands. Divide the strands between the two prepared baking sheets, drizzle with the olive oil, season and toss to coat.

STEP THREE Roast for about 20 minutes, until crisp and lightly golden, turning them over halfway through the cooking time so that they cook evenly.

TIP
Try 'spiralising' peeled parsnips or butternut squash, and baking them as above.

STUFFED VEGGIE POTATOES

PREP: 10 MINS
COOK: 1 HOUR 15 MINS

3 medium baking potatoes
a knob of butter
50g (2 oz) leeks, sliced
75g (3 oz) broccoli florets
50g (2 oz) Cheddar
  cheese, grated
9 cherry tomatoes, halved
salt and black pepper

Baked potatoes are a great standby when the cupboard is bare, and these ones are super-tasty. If you have ham to hand, make a meaty version by chopping it and adding it to the vegetable mix or scattering it over the potatoes with the cherry tomatoes and cheese.

STEP ONE Preheat the oven to 200°C/400°F/Gas 6.

STEP TWO Prick the potatoes with the prongs of a fork, and bake them in the oven, directly on the oven shelf, for about 1 hour, until their skins are crisp and they are soft in the middle, or cook them in the microwave on High for 7–10 minutes. Leave to cool slightly, then slice in half and scoop out most of the potato flesh from each half into a bowl, being sure to keep the skin intact. Add the knob of butter to the bowl, mash and season to taste.

STEP THREE Cook the leek and broccoli in boiling water for 3 minutes. Drain, then mash with a potato masher. Add to the bowl of potato with half of the grated cheese and mix together. Spoon the mixture back into the potato shells.

STEP FOUR Arrange three halved cherry tomatoes on top of each potato and sprinkle with the remaining cheese. Put the stuffed halved potatoes into a shallow roasting tin and bake in the oven for 10–15 minutes, or until crisp and the cheese has melted. If you like, pop the potatoes under a preheated grill for a couple of minutes to brown the tops.

ROASTED CAULIFLOWER

PREP: 5 MINS
COOK: 25 MINS

1 large cauliflower, cut
    into small florets
2 tbsp olive oil
salt and black pepper

FOR THE DRESSING
1½ tbsp rice wine vinegar
½ tsp runny honey
2 tbsp olive oil
1 tbsp chopped fresh
    parsley leaves (optional),
    plus extra to garnish

Steamed cauliflower is fine, but I urge you to try it roasted instead. Eating it cooked this way can transform a picky eater into a confirmed cauliflower addict. The edges brown and caramelise, and the cauliflower takes on a delicious nutty, buttery flavour. It's great on its own, or drizzled with this honey and rice wine vinegar dressing.

STEP ONE Preheat the oven to 200°C/400°F/Gas 6.

STEP TWO Arrange the cauliflower florets on a baking tray. Add the olive oil, toss and season well. Roast for 25 minutes, until golden.

STEP THREE Whisk the dressing ingredients together in a small bowl. Drizzle the dressing over the roasted cauliflower, scatter with extra parsley (if using) and serve warm.

TIP
Sprinkle the cauliflower with grated Parmesan cheese 5 minutes before the end of roasting time, or sprinkle with smoked paprika or ground cumin before roasting.

COURGETTE 'SPAGHETTI'

PREP: 5 MINS
COOK: 6 MINS

4 large courgettes
3 tbsp olive oil
2–3 garlic cloves, crushed
250 g (9 oz) cherry
   tomatoes, halved
2 tbsp fresh green pesto
50 g (2 oz) Parmesan
   cheese, grated
salt and black pepper

Spiralisers are easy to use, and magically transforming veggies into 'spaghetti' is a fantastic way to tempt fussy eaters. In fact, get them to help you and join in the fun.

STEP ONE Put the courgettes through a spiraliser to make long spaghetti-like strands.

STEP TWO Heat 2 tablespoons of the olive oil in a large frying pan over a medium heat. Add the garlic and fry for a few seconds, then add the spiralised courgettes to the pan. Toss over a high heat for 2–3 minutes, until just softening, then remove and set aside on kitchen paper.

STEP THREE Return the frying pan to the heat, add the remaining olive oil, then fry the tomatoes for 2 minutes. Season, add the spiralised courgettes, pesto and grated Parmesan, toss until heated through and serve immediately.

CURRIED SWEETCORN FRITTERS

PREP: 25 MINS
COOK: 20 MINS

2 x 150 g (5 oz) cans
    sweetcorn, drained
1 bunch spring onions, sliced
2 tbsp korma curry paste
1 tbsp mango chutney
1 large egg
6 tbsp whole milk
200 g (7 oz) plain flour
sunflower oil, for frying
salt and black pepper

FOR THE SALSA
(OPTIONAL)
2 large tomatoes, deseeded
    and finely diced
½ cucumber, deseeded
    and finely diced
½ red onion, finely diced
1 tbsp rice wine vinegar
1–2 tbsp mango chutney
    (to taste)

Korma curry paste gives these sweetcorn fritters an added flavour boost. They are best eaten straight away, on their own or with an optional salsa or dip, or you can cook half the mixture, keeping the rest in the fridge for the next day.

STEP ONE Put half the drained sweetcorn in the bowl of a food processor with the spring onions, curry paste and mango chutney. Blitz until roughly chopped, then add the egg, milk, flour and some salt and pepper. Blend until combined. Remove the bowl from the food processor and stir in the reserved sweetcorn.

STEP TWO Heat 4 tablespoons of sunflower oil in a frying pan (just enough to cover the base), then carefully drop tablespoons of the sweetcorn mixture into the hot oil and fry for about 4 minutes, until golden brown and crisp, turning them after 2 minutes to cook on the other side. Remove and leave to drain on kitchen paper while you cook the remaining fritters.

STEP THREE Mix all the salsa ingredients together, if using, season to taste, and serve alongside the fritters.

Makes 3–4 portions

GRIDDLED COURGETTES WITH BALSAMIC GLAZE

PREP: 12 MINS
COOK: 20 MINS

3 large courgettes, trimmed
    and thinly sliced lengthways
    with a vegetable peeler
4 tbsp olive oil
2 tbsp balsamic glaze
1 small garlic clove, crushed
pecorino or Parmesan cheese,
    shaved, to serve
salt and black pepper

To make griddled courgettes you need a smoking-hot griddle pan so that you get those lovely black char lines. Serve with shavings of pecorino or Parmesan cheese.

STEP ONE Put the courgette strips into a resealable plastic bag. Add 2 tablespoons of the olive oil and season. Close the bag and shake it so that the courgette strips are covered in oil.

STEP TWO Heat a griddle pan over a high heat. Once it's smoking hot, griddle the courgettes in batches until just soft, flipping them over to cook both sides, but being careful not to move them around too much (otherwise you won't get those lovely char marks). Remove and arrange on a plate.

STEP THREE Combine the remaining oil with the balsamic glaze and garlic, and drizzle the glaze over the courgettes. Serve with shavings of pecorino or Parmesan.

Makes 4 portions

GARLIC AND CHILLI PRAWNS

PREP: 6 MINS
COOK: 5 MINS

1½ tbsp olive oil
2 garlic cloves, finely chopped
½–1 red chilli, deseeded
  and finely sliced
8 raw king prawns, shell on
juice of ½ lemon
salt and black pepper

The beauty of prawns is that they take only minutes to cook, and this is a delicious way to serve them, either as a starter or as part of a main dish.

STEP ONE Heat the olive oil in a large frying pan or wok over a high heat until very hot. Add the garlic and chilli, then add the prawns. Sauté over a high heat, stirring, for 4–5 minutes until the prawns have turned pink and are cooked through. Season, add the lemon juice and serve immediately.

TIP
To remove the smell of garlic from your hands, put a little salt or baking soda on them and rub them together, then rinse under cold water. Alternatively, rub your hands across a stainless steel utensil under cold running water.

Chapter three
PREPARE AHEAD

*Makes 4–6 portions
(freezer friendly)*

CHILLED ROAST TOMATO SOUP

**PREP: 20 MINS
COOK: 30–40 MINS**

1–1.5 kg (2¼–3¼ lb) sweet,
    ripe cherry tomatoes, halved
200 g (7 oz) soft, sundried
    tomatoes, roughly chopped
1–2 red onions, roughly
    chopped
4 garlic cloves, roughly
    chopped
3 tbsp chopped fresh
    basil leaves
2 tbsp chopped parsley stalks,
    and a few chopped leaves
2 tbsp olive oil
300 ml (½ pint) vegetable stock
    or water
balsamic vinegar, to taste
rocket, mozzarella or croutons,
    to serve (optional)
crème fraîche, to serve
    (optional)
salt and black pepper

This sweet, vibrant soup is packed full of delicious Italian flavours. Try it cold – you might be pleasantly surprised.

STEP ONE Preheat the oven to 200°C/400°F/Gas 6.

STEP TWO Place the fresh and sundried tomatoes in a large roasting tin with the onions, garlic and herbs, season, drizzle with the olive oil and roast for 30–40 minutes, until the skin of the tomatoes blister and the onions and garlic have softened. Remove from the oven and leave to cool, then discard some of the larger chunks of garlic and blitz it all in blender until smooth.

STEP THREE Pass the soup through a sieve into a large bowl, to remove the tomato seeds and skin, making sure you don't leave any soup behind (I do this by adding a bit of the vegetable stock or water to the sieve, to help loosen the remaining mixture).

STEP FOUR Stir in the rest of the stock or water to thin it slightly, then chill until ready to serve. Add a little balsamic vinegar, to taste, then garnish with rocket, mozzarella, croutons or crème fraîche, or just leave it as it is!

Makes 4–6 portions (freezer friendly)

PREP: 25 MINS
COOK: 40 MINS

2 tbsp olive oil
1 large onion, finely chopped
2 garlic cloves, crushed
2 x 400 g (14 oz) cans
   chopped tomatoes
2 tbsp tomato purée
½ tsp dried oregano
a pinch of caster sugar
225 g (8 oz) fusilli
2 tbsp chopped fresh
   basil leaves
125 g (4½ oz) mozzarella,
   sliced
50 g (2 oz) mature Cheddar
   cheese, grated
salt and black pepper

FOR THE MEATBALLS
350 g (12 oz) lean minced beef
50 g (2 oz) fresh white
   breadcrumbs
50 g (2 oz) Parmesan cheese,
   grated
1 egg yolk
1 tbsp chopped fresh
   thyme leaves

PASTA MEATBALL BAKE

Jazz up your weeknight pasta bakes with some meatballs. Make sure to sprinkle some mozzarella and Cheddar cheese on top, for that bubbling, golden coating.

STEP ONE Place all of the meatball ingredients in a bowl. Season well and mix together. Shape into 20 balls.

STEP TWO Heat the olive oil in a saucepan over a medium heat. Brown the meatballs in batches, then set aside. Add the onion and garlic to the pan and sauté for 5 minutes. Add the tomatoes, tomato purée, dried oregano and sugar and bring to the boil. Return the meatballs to the pan and simmer uncovered for 15 minutes, until cooked through.

STEP THREE Meanwhile, cook the pasta in a large saucepan of lightly salted boiling water according to the packet instructions. Drain and add to the sauce with the basil leaves.

STEP FOUR Preheat the grill. Spoon the pasta with meatballs into a heatproof dish. Sprinkle with the sliced and grated cheeses. Grill for 10 minutes, until melted and golden brown.

Makes 4 portions (freezer friendly)

AUBERGINE PARMIGIANA

PREP: 25 MINS
COOK: 1 HOUR

4 large aubergines
   (about 1 kg/2¼ lb)
3 large eggs, beaten
100 g (4 oz) plain flour
250 g (9 oz) mozzarella
   balls, sliced
100 g (4 oz) Parmesan
   cheese, grated
1 small bunch fresh basil
   leaves, chopped
salt and black pepper

FOR THE SAUCE
2 tbsp olive oil, plus extra
   for frying and greasing
2 onions, chopped
2 garlic cloves, crushed
3 x 400 g (14 oz) cans
   chopped tomatoes
1 tsp caster sugar

I love this classic north Italian dish, with layers of aubergine, mozzarella and tomato. For me, it's Mediterranean comfort food at its best.

STEP ONE Preheat the oven to 200°C/400°F/Gas 6.

STEP TWO To make the sauce, heat the olive oil in a large saucepan over a medium heat. Add the onions and garlic and sauté for 5 minutes until soft. Add the tomatoes and sugar, then cover and simmer for 20 minutes. Season.

STEP THREE Place the beaten eggs in a wide, shallow bowl and the flour in a separate wide, shallow bowl, and heat a little oil in a large frying pan. Cut the aubergines widthways into 12 mm- (½ in-) thick slices. Dip them into the beaten egg, then into the flour, to coat. Fry the aubergine slices, in batches, for 2 minutes on each side until golden brown and crisp on both sides, then drain on kitchen paper.

STEP FOUR To assemble the parmigiana, spread a thin layer of tomato sauce over the base of a large greased ovenproof dish. Put a layer of fried aubergine on top, then put a third of the sliced mozzarella balls and a third of the Parmesan cheese on top, followed by some chopped basil leaves. Repeat, seasoning each layer, until you have four layers of aubergine and cheeses and three layers of sauce (the aubergine and cheeses being the top layer).

STEP FIVE Bake for 30 minutes, until piping hot and bubbling.

MOROCCAN CHICKEN WITH BUTTERNUT SQUASH AND RED ONION COUSCOUS

PREP: 20 MINS
COOK: 40–50 MINS

2 tbsp olive oil

1 kg (2¼ lb) boneless, skinless chicken thighs, cut into chunks

2 large shallots, chopped

2 carrots, diced

2 celery sticks, sliced

3 garlic cloves, crushed

2 tsp ground ginger

2 tsp ground coriander

2 tsp ground cumin

½ tsp ground cinnamon

300 ml (½ pint) chicken stock

400 g (14 oz) can chopped tomatoes

1–2 tbsp runny honey (to taste)

350 g (12 oz) butternut squash, peeled, deseeded and cubed

juice of 1 small lemon

salt and black pepper

FOR THE RED ONION COUSCOUS

300 g (11 oz) couscous

600 ml (1 pint) hot chicken or vegetable stock

1 tsp ground turmeric

1 tbsp olive oil

1 bunch mint leaves, chopped

1 bunch parsley leaves, chopped

3 red onions, sliced

1 tsp caster sugar

juice of ½ lemon

This fragrant chicken recipe is simple to prepare as everything is cooked in one pot. Any leftover couscous makes for an ideal packed lunch the next day.

STEP ONE Heat half of the olive oil in a deep, lidded frying pan. Season the chicken, then fry in the oil until lightly golden. Remove from the pan and set aside.

STEP TWO Heat the remaining olive oil in the pan. Add the shallots, carrot and celery and sauté for 5 minutes, then add the garlic and all the ground spices and sauté for a further minute.

STEP THREE Add the stock, chopped tomatoes, honey and chicken. Bring to the boil, cover and simmer for 30–40 minutes until the chicken is cooked through and tender. Add the cubed squash after 15 minutes.

STEP FOUR Meanwhile, make the red onion couscous. Place the couscous in a bowl. Pour over the hot stock and turmeric, stir, then cover with clingfilm and leave to soak for 20 minutes. While it's soaking, heat the olive oil in a frying pan over a medium heat. Add the onion and sugar and sauté, stirring, until soft and golden brown. Leave to cool, then remove the clingfilm from the bowl of couscous, fluff up with a fork, stir in the chopped herbs, onion and lemon juice, and season well.

STEP FIVE Add the lemon juice to the chicken and season well to taste. Serve with the fluffy couscous.

Makes 4 portions

MEDITERRANEAN OVEN-BAKED CHICKEN DRUMSTICKS

PREP: 12 MINS
COOK: 45 MINS

8 chicken drumsticks or
    4 large chicken thighs
    (skin on)
2 tbsp olive oil
2 garlic cloves, crushed
1 red onion, thickly sliced
1 red pepper, deseeded and
    finely chopped
500 g (1 lb 2 oz) tomato passata
2 tbsp sundried tomato paste
salt and black pepper
fresh basil leaves, to garnish

This deliciously moist, baked chicken dish is infused with the taste of the Med, and takes only moments to assemble.

STEP ONE Preheat the oven to 200°C/400°F/Gas 6.

STEP TWO Score each chicken leg or thigh a few times with a sharp knife and drizzle with the olive oil. Rub the garlic into the chicken, then place it in a roasting tin or ovenproof dish. Roast for 20 minutes.

STEP THREE Add the onion and pepper to the roasting tin and bake for a further 15 minutes, until just softened.

STEP FOUR Mix the passata with the sundried tomato paste and pour it over the chicken and vegetables. Season and bake for a further 10 minutes, until bubbling. Sprinkle with the basil leaves and serve.

Makes 4 portions

STICKY COCONUT CHICKEN THIGHS

PREP: 10 MINS
COOK: 40–45 MINS

8 large or 4 small chicken
 thighs (skin on)
200 ml (7 fl oz) coconut milk
3 garlic cloves, crushed
grated zest and juice of ½ lime
2 lemongrass stalks, bashed
½–1 red chilli, deseeded
 and diced
2 tbsp sweet chilli sauce
1 tbsp soy sauce
2 tbsp chopped fresh
 coriander leaves
salt and black pepper

Coated in a Thai-inspired blend of coconut milk, lemongrass, garlic and lime, these chicken thighs make a perfect weekend treat, served with fluffy jasmine rice and steamed pak choi.

STEP ONE Preheat the oven to 200°C/400°F/Gas 6.

STEP TWO Put the chicken thighs in a roasting tin and season. Mix the coconut milk, crushed garlic and lime zest together and pour the mixture over the thighs, then add the bashed lemongrass stalks. Cover with foil and roast for 20 minutes.

STEP THREE Mix the diced chilli, lime juice, sweet chilli sauce and soy sauce together in a bowl. Remove the roasting tin from the oven, take off the foil and pour over the chilli mixture. Roast uncovered for 20–25 minutes, basting occasionally, until the chicken is golden brown, crisp and cooked through.

STEP FOUR Discard the lemongrass stalks and sprinkle with coriander to serve.

CHICKEN, BACON AND TOMATO LASAGNE

PREP: 10 MINS
COOK: 35-40 MINS

1 tbsp olive oil
1 large onion, roughly chopped
4 rashers smoked back
   bacon, chopped
2 garlic cloves, crushed
2 skinless chicken breasts,
   cut into thin strips
2 x 400 g (14 oz) cans
   chopped tomatoes
2 tbsp sundried tomato paste
1 tbsp chopped fresh
   thyme leaves
6 fresh lasagne sheets
salt and black pepper

FOR THE CHEESE SAUCE
50 g (2 oz) butter
50 g (2 oz) plain flour
450 ml (¾ pint) whole milk
1 tsp Dijon mustard
100 g (4 oz) Cheddar
   cheese, grated

Try this twist on a classic lasagne. The chicken and bacon blend brings a great smoky flavour to each mouthful. Serve with a vibrant green salad.

STEP ONE Preheat the oven to 180°C/350°F/Gas 4.

STEP TWO Heat the olive oil in a large frying pan, add the onion and bacon, and sauté until the onion is soft. Add the garlic and chicken and fry for a few minutes until browned. Add the chopped tomatoes, tomato paste and chopped thyme. Bring to the boil, season, then simmer uncovered for 5 minutes.

STEP THREE To make the cheese sauce, melt the butter in a saucepan, add the flour and cook for 1 minute, stirring continuously. Gradually whisk in the milk, bring to the boil, then simmer and stir until thickened and smooth. Remove from the heat, add the mustard and three-quarters of the grated cheese, and season to taste.

STEP FOUR To assemble the lasagne, spoon a third of the chicken sauce onto the base of an ovenproof dish. Cover with two sheets of lasagne. Spread over a third of the cheese sauce. Repeat with the remaining lasagne sheets and sauces, making sure that the top layer is the cheese sauce. Sprinkle with the reserved grated cheese and bake for 25–30 minutes, until brown and bubbling. Leave to stand for 5 minutes before serving.

TIP
Before cutting pancetta or bacon, put it in the freezer for no more than a minute. This will firm up the meat and make it easier to cut.

*Makes 4 portions
(freezer friendly)*

**PREP: 12 MINS
COOK: 25 MINS**

2 tbsp olive oil
1 onion, chopped
2 small carrots, finely diced
1 celery stick, finely diced
1 garlic clove, crushed
375 g (13 oz) sausagemeat
2 x 400 g (14 oz) cans
   chopped tomatoes
2 tbsp sundried tomato paste
1 tbsp chopped fresh
   thyme leaves
275 g (10 oz) fusilli
salt and black pepper
Parmesan cheese, grated,
   to serve (optional)

SAUSAGE RAGÙ

This is a winning recipe for all the family. Use the best-quality sausagemeat you can get hold of, to give the dish its deep, savoury flavour.

STEP ONE Heat the olive oil in a saucepan or frying pan, add the onion, carrot, celery and garlic and sauté for 2–3 minutes, until soft. Add the sausagemeat, breaking it up with a wooden spoon, and let it brown with the vegetables.

STEP TWO Add the chopped tomatoes, sundried tomato paste and thyme. Season and simmer, covered, for about 20 minutes, until the sauce has reduced and thickened.

STEP THREE Meanwhile, cook the pasta in a large saucepan of lightly salted boiling water according to the packet instructions. Drain the pasta and add it to the sauce. Toss to combine, and serve sprinkled with Parmesan cheese, if you like.

Makes 6 portions

ROAST LOIN OF PORK WITH ROAST POTATOES AND GRAVY

PREP: 20 MINS
COOK: 1–1½ HOURS

2 red onions, peeled and
    cut into wedges
1.3 kg (2¾ lb) boned
    loin of pork, at room
    temperature, skin scored
    with a sharp knife
6 medium potatoes, peeled
    and cut into large chunks
2 tbsp olive oil
3 dessert apples, cored and
    thickly sliced (unpeeled)
1 bunch sage leaves
salt and black pepper

FOR THE GRAVY
2 tbsp plain flour
100 ml (3½ fl oz) dry sherry
500 ml (7 fl oz) chicken stock
sprinkle of caster sugar
1 tsp Worcestershire sauce

A delicious recipe for succulent roast pork, which I like to serve with a tasty gravy made with the roasting tin juices.

STEP ONE Preheat the oven to 200°C/400°F/Gas 6.

STEP TWO Place the onion wedges in the base of a roasting tin. Put the pork on top, then scatter the potatoes around the pork. Drizzle the potatoes with the olive oil and season, then rub salt into the pork skin.

STEP THREE Roast for 1–1½ hours, until golden and crisp and the pork and potatoes are cooked through, adding the apple slices and sage after 30 minutes of cooking time has passed.

STEP FOUR Remove the pork from the tin, making sure that no pink juices are running from the meat, and set aside to rest, covered with foil. Remove the potatoes, apple and onion from the tin, too.

STEP FIVE To make the gravy, place the roasting tin on the hob over a medium heat. Skim away any excess fat. Add the flour, stir for a minute, then add the sherry, stock, sugar and Worcestershire sauce and simmer, stirring, until thickened. Serve with the pork, apple and roast potatoes.

TIP
To ensure crispy crackling, pat the skin of the pork dry with some kitchen paper before cooking. And leave plenty of time for the meat to rest after roasting: this makes the meat more tender.

Makes 6 portions (freezer friendly)

**PREP: 20 MINS
COOK: 40 MINS**

2 tbsp olive oil
2 onions, chopped
1 garlic clove, crushed
85 g (3½ oz) fresh
    white breadcrumbs
6 tbsp whole milk
1 tbsp chopped fresh
    thyme leaves
1 carrot, grated
½ dessert apple, peeled
    and grated
500 g (1 lb 2 oz) lean
    minced beef
2 tbsp tomato ketchup
1 tbsp Worcestershire sauce
2 tsp runny honey
salt and black pepper

FOR THE TOMATO SAUCE
400 g (14 oz) can
    chopped tomatoes
2 tbsp tomato ketchup
1 tsp Worcestershire sauce
2 tsp runny honey

MEATLOAF

Adding the sauce to the meatloaf gives the finished dish an appealing appearance. Serve with roast potatoes and steamed vegetables.

STEP ONE Preheat the oven to 180°C/350°F/Gas 4 and line the base and sides of a 900 g (2 lb) loaf tin with non-stick baking paper.

STEP TWO Heat the olive oil in a saucepan and sauté the onion and garlic until soft. Remove from the heat and leave to cool.

STEP THREE Put half of the cooked onion and garlic into a large mixing bowl. Add the remaining ingredients. Season and mix together thoroughly. Spoon into the prepared tin and level the top. Bake for 40 minutes, or until golden brown and cooked through.

STEP FOUR Just before the meatloaf is cooked, put the remaining cooked onion and garlic into a saucepan. Add the chopped tomatoes, tomato ketchup, Worcestershire sauce and honey. Bring to the boil, then simmer for 3–4 minutes.

STEP FIVE Transfer the meatloaf from the tin to a serving plate and pour over the tomato sauce to serve.

MINCED BEEF CROQUETTES

PREP: 30 MINS
COOK: 30–35 MINS

400 g (14 oz) floury potatoes,
    peeled and cut into
    small chunks
2 tbsp sunflower oil
25 g (1 oz) butter
1 onion, finely chopped
250 g (9 oz) lean minced beef
2 tsp chopped fresh
    thyme leaves
1 tbsp chopped fresh
    parsley leaves
1 tbsp tomato ketchup
1 tsp Worcestershire sauce
a little plain flour, for dusting
salt and black pepper

FOR THE GRAVY
1 tbsp sunflower oil
1 onion, thinly sliced
1 tsp demerara sugar
1 beef stock cube
1 tbsp cornflour
1 tsp tomato purée
a few drops of Worcestershire
    sauce

TIP
When making mashed potato, after
you drain the potatoes, return them
to the hot pan, cover tightly and let
them steam for a few minutes. This
allows the potatoes to dry out so
they'll mash perfectly and soak up
the butter more easily.

These scrumptious beef croquettes and tasty onion gravy are a match made in heaven. You could use leftover roast beef, chopped for a few seconds in a food processor, instead of minced beef. Simply sauté the onion and thyme, then stir in the chopped roast beef and mix with the remaining ingredients.

STEP ONE Cook the potatoes in a large pan of lightly salted boiling water for 15 minutes, or until tender, then drain and mash with the butter. Set aside to cool.

STEP TWO Heat 1 tablespoon of the sunflower oil with the butter in a saucepan and sauté the onion for 3–4 minutes. Add the minced beef and sauté for a further 3–4 minutes, then stir in the thyme and season. Cook for a minute more, then transfer to a large bowl. Stir the cooled potato into the beef with the parsley, ketchup and Worcestershire sauce, and season to taste. Cover and leave in the fridge until cold.

STEP THREE Using your hands, shape the beef and potato mixture into 12 logs. Roll each log in flour, transfer to a plate and chill for at least 1 hour. Once chilled, heat the remaining oil in a large frying pan and sauté the croquettes in batches for 5–8 minutes, turning them frequently, until crisp and golden brown. Drain on kitchen paper.

STEP FOUR To make the gravy, heat the sunflower oil in a saucepan over a low heat, and sauté the onion until soft. Stir in the demerara sugar. Dissolve the stock cube in 400 ml (13 fl oz) boiling water, then mix 1 tablespoon of cold water with the cornflour and stir it into the beef stock. Pour the stock into the saucepan with the onion, stir in the tomato purée and Worcestershire sauce. Bring to the boil and simmer for 3–4 minutes, until thickened. Season to taste and serve with the croquettes.

LAMB BURGERS
WITH SALSA

**PREP: 25 MINS
COOK: 20 MINS**

1 tbsp olive oil
4 large pitta breads
a little mayonnaise,
    for spreading
1 large carrot, grated

FOR THE BURGERS
500 g (1 lb 2 oz) minced lamb
4 tbsp chopped fresh
    parsley leaves
1 onion, finely chopped
1 tsp ground cumin
½ tsp ground coriander
50 g (2 oz) fresh white
    breadcrumbs
1 egg yolk
salt and black pepper

FOR THE SALSA
100 g (4 oz) cucumber, peeled,
    quartered lengthways,
    deseeded and thinly sliced
100 g (4 oz) cherry tomatoes,
    quartered
2 spring onions, sliced
1 tbsp rice wine vinegar
1 tbsp olive oil
1 tbsp chopped fresh
    mint leaves

These spiced, juicy lamb burgers make a great barbecue dish, or work just as well cooked under the grill. Serve in toasted pitta bread with a zingy tomato, cucumber and mint salsa.

STEP ONE Place the burger ingredients in the bowl of a food processor. Whizz briefly until combined, then season generously and shape the mixture into 8 burgers. Alternatively, mix by hand then shape into burgers.

STEP TWO Heat the olive oil in a frying pan over a medium heat. Add the lamb burgers and fry in batches for 3–4 minutes on each side, until browned and cooked through.

STEP THREE Toast the pitta breads and slice each pitta in half to make 8 small pockets. Spread a little mayonnaise inside each pitta bread pocket. Place a burger inside each pocket, then add a little grated carrot. To make the salsa, mix the vegetables together, then dress with the vinegar and oil, add the mint, and spoon on top of the grated carrot to serve.

CHILLI BEEF CASSEROLE

PREP: 15 MINS
COOK: 1½–2 HOURS

2 tbsp olive oil
1 kg (2¼ lb) braising
   steak, diced
2 large onions, sliced
1 red pepper, deseeded
   and diced
2 garlic cloves, crushed
1 tbsp ground cumin
1 tbsp ground coriander
¼ tsp Spanish sweet
   smoked paprika
300 ml (½ pint) white wine
400 g (14 oz) can chopped
   tomatoes
3 tbsp tomato purée
1 tbsp mango chutney
400 g (14 oz) can red kidney
   beans, drained and rinsed
salt and black pepper

This dish boasts a fabulous combination of flavours –
I love the hint of sweetness from the smoked paprika
and the mango chutney. If your child isn't keen on
kidney beans, add a can of drained cannellini beans
instead. Serve this with rice and grated cheese,
sour cream and guacamole.

STEP ONE Heat the olive oil in a flameproof casserole
over a medium heat. Brown the beef in batches, then
set aside.

STEP TWO Once all the beef is browned, add the
onions, pepper and garlic to the casserole and sauté
for 3 minutes. Add the spices, then stir in the wine,
chopped tomatoes, tomato purée and mango chutney.
Return the beef to the pan, bring to the boil, season,
cover and simmer gently on the hob, or in a preheated
oven (150°C/300°F/Gas 2), for 1½–2 hours, until the
beef is tender.

STEP THREE Add the drained kidney beans to
the casserole 30 minutes before the end of the
cooking time.

TIP
Cook double batches of soups,
casseroles and stews and
freeze half for another time.

PREP: 20 MINS
COOK: 20 MINS

500 g (1 lb 2 oz) minced turkey
50 g (2 oz) fresh white
    breadcrumbs
1 red onion, chopped
1 small garlic clove, crushed
1 tbsp chopped fresh
    thyme leaves
4 tbsp tomato ketchup
1 tbsp Worcestershire sauce
a little olive oil, for frying
salt and black pepper

TURKEY MEATLOAF MEATBALLS

Serve up a hearty helping of these moist turkey meatballs with some buttery mash and onion gravy (see page 144) or opt for pasta.

STEP ONE Place all of the ingredients apart from the oil into the bowl of a food processor. Whizz for a few seconds until combined, then season and roll into about 25 balls. Alternatively, mix by hand then shape into balls.

STEP TWO Heat a little oil in a frying pan. Add the balls and fry in batches for 4–5 minutes, turning occasionally, until golden brown and cooked through.

TIP
Open-freeze the uncooked meatballs on a lined baking tray before transferring to a labelled plastic food bag. Defrost thoroughly before cooking.

Makes 4–6 portions (freezer friendly)

CURRIED BEEF GOULASH

PREP: 12 MINS
COOK: 2 HOURS

2 tbsp olive oil
900 g (2 lb) diced braising
    steak
2 onions, sliced
1 red pepper, deseeded
    and diced
2 garlic cloves, crushed
2 cm (¾ in) piece of fresh root
    ginger, peeled and grated
2 tbsp mild curry paste
2 tsp garam masala
2 tsp ground cumin
2 tsp ground coriander
2 x 400 g (14 oz) cans
    chopped tomatoes
1 tbsp mango chutney
juice of ½ lime
salt and black pepper
fresh coriander leaves,
    chopped, to serve

This mild, tomato-based goulash of lovely, tender beef tastes even better eaten the day after it is cooked. Serve with long-grain rice.

STEP ONE Heat the olive oil in a flameproof casserole over a medium heat and brown the beef in batches. Transfer the browned beef to a plate and set aside.

STEP TWO Add the onion and pepper to the casserole and sauté for 3 minutes, then add the garlic and ginger, spices and the browned beef. Add the chopped tomatoes, mango chutney and season. Bring to the boil, cover and simmer gently on the hob over a low heat, or in a preheated oven (150°C/300°F/Gas 2), for 1½–2 hours, stirring occasionally and adding a little water if it looks too dry, until the beef is tender.

STEP THREE Stir in the lime juice and scatter with coriander leaves just before serving.

Makes 4 portions (freezer friendly)

SALMON AND COD GRATIN

PREP: 15 MINS
COOK: 15 MINS

40 g (1½ oz) butter

150 g (5 oz) leek, trimmed
    and sliced

40 g (1½ oz) plain flour

600 ml (1 pint) whole milk

1 tbsp Dijon mustard

1 tbsp lemon juice

30 g (1¼ oz) Parmesan
    cheese, grated

70 g (2½ oz) Cheddar
    cheese, grated

400 g (14 oz) boneless and
    skinless salmon and cod
    fillets, cubed

1 tbsp chopped fresh dill

200 g (7 oz) carrot, cut into
    small dice

175 g (6 oz) potato, peeled
    and cut into small dice

salt and black pepper

I call this my deconstructed fish pie. It's a delicious combination of salmon and cod with cubes of carrot and potato in a cheesy dill sauce with a gratinéed cheese topping.

STEP ONE Melt the butter in a saucepan, add the leek and sauté for 3–4 minutes until soft. Add the flour and stir over the heat for 1 minute. Gradually whisk in the milk, bring to the boil and stir continuously until thickened.

STEP TWO Add the Dijon mustard, lemon juice, Parmesan, and 40 g (1½ oz) of the grated Cheddar cheese. Add the fish and simmer gently for 3–4 minutes, then remove from the heat and stir in the chopped dill.

STEP THREE Meanwhile, cook the carrots and potatoes together in lightly salted boiling water for 10 minutes, then drain. Stir them into the cheese sauce and season. Preheat the grill.

STEP FOUR Spoon the fish mixture into a large ovenproof dish. Sprinkle over the remaining Cheddar and grill for 5–7 minutes until golden.

Chapter four

LUNCHBOXES AND SNACKS

Makes 4 portions

BANG BANG CHICKEN SALAD

PREP: 15 MINS
COOK: 10 MINS

125 g (4½ oz) medium
   egg noodles
1 bunch spring onions, sliced
½ cucumber, peeled, deseeded
   and sliced into crescent-
   shaped chunks
1 carrot, thinly sliced
   into strips
2 small Little Gem lettuces,
   leaves separated
2 skinless chicken breasts,
   sliced into strips
1 tbsp sweet chilli sauce
2 tbsp sunflower oil
salt and black pepper

FOR THE DRESSING
1 tbsp rice wine vinegar
3 tbsp olive oil
2 tbsp sweet chilli sauce
2 tbsp smooth peanut butter

A refreshing, crunchy salad layered with noodles and chicken. Great for peanut butter lovers.

STEP ONE Cook the noodles in a large saucepan of lightly salted boiling water according to the packet instructions. Drain and refresh under cold water, then cut into short lengths.

STEP TWO Put the spring onions, cucumber and carrot in a large bowl, and add the drained noodles.

STEP THREE Whisk together all the ingredients for the dressing with 3 tablespoons of water in a small bowl. Toss the salad with half of the dressing and season to taste.

STEP FOUR Arrange the lettuce leaves in a serving bowl and top with the noodle salad.

STEP FIVE Mix the chicken with the sweet chilli sauce. Heat the oil in a frying pan over a high heat. Fry the chicken strips for a few minutes, until cooked through.

STEP SIX Scatter the chicken on top of the noodles, and drizzle over the remaining dressing.

Makes 4–6 portions

CHICKEN, CHERRY TOMATO AND MOZZARELLA SALAD

PREP: 15 MINS
COOK: 10 MINS

75 g (3 oz) ciabatta bread,
   cut into chunks
2 tbsp olive oil
2 Cos lettuces, thickly sliced
150 g (5 oz) cherry tomatoes,
   halved
¼ cucumber, peeled,
   deseeded and sliced into
   crescent- shaped chunks
1 cooked skinless chicken
   breast, sliced
30 g (1¼ oz) Parmesan
   cheese, grated
125 g (4½ oz) mini
   mozzarella balls
salt and black pepper

FOR THE DRESSING
2 tbsp balsamic vinegar
6 tbsp olive oil
½ tsp Dijon mustard

A popular Italian dish that all of the family can enjoy. You can substitute ciabatta for another kind of Italian bread.

STEP ONE Preheat the oven to 200°C/400°F/Gas 6.

STEP TWO Toss the ciabatta chunks with the olive oil, place on a baking sheet and bake for 10 minutes, until crisp. Remove from the oven and set aside to cool.

STEP THREE Place the lettuce in a large serving bowl, add the remaining salad ingredients and toss together.

STEP FOUR Whisk all of the dressing ingredients together in a small bowl and pour the dressing over the salad. Scatter over the ciabatta croutons, season and serve.

Makes 6 portions

CRUNCHY SWEETCORN SALSA SALAD

PREP: 15 MINS

2 carrots, finely diced
1 red pepper, deseeded
  and diced
326 g (11 oz) can sweetcorn,
  drained
1 small red onion, chopped
50 g (2 oz) pine nuts, toasted
salt and black pepper

FOR THE DRESSING
3 tbsp olive oil
1½ tsp Dijon mustard
1 tbsp white wine vinegar

I love the nutty taste of sweetcorn, and the sweet red pepper and toasted pine nuts add some crunch to this refreshing salad.

STEP ONE Place all of the ingredients for the salad into a large serving bowl.

STEP TWO Whisk the dressing ingredients together, then pour them over the salad. Mix and season well.

TIP
To toast the pine nuts, put them on a baking tray and dry-roast in a hot oven for a few minutes, giving the tray a shake halfway through, or toast in a dry frying pan until golden.

CHERYL'S POWER SEED BARS

PREP: 20 MINS
COOK: 4 HOURS, 30 MINS

350 g (12 oz) low-cholesterol margarine, plus extra for greasing
40 g (1½ oz) Splenda or stevia
3 large eggs, lightly beaten
284 ml (10 fl oz) carton buttermilk
250 g (9 oz) Bran Flakes
150 g (5 oz) Grape Nuts
750 g (1 lb 10 oz) self-raising flour
5 tsp baking powder
1 tsp salt
50 g (2 oz) sunflower seeds
30 g (1¼ oz) chia seeds
50 g (2 oz) linseeds or flaxseeds

My South African friend Cheryl makes the most amazing, healthy but delicious rusks. The Stevia and margarine make them lower in calories than most energy bars, but if you prefer, use caster sugar and butter instead. You can also vary them by adding dried fruit such as raisins, and they will keep for a month in an airtight container.

STEP ONE Preheat the oven to 160°C/325°F/Gas 3 and lightly grease a 38 x 26 cm (15 x 10 in) baking tin.

STEP TWO Melt the margarine in a large saucepan over a low heat, then add the Splenda or stevia.

STEP THREE Mix the eggs in a bowl with the buttermilk.

STEP FOUR Put all the dry ingredients in a separate large bowl, then stir in the melted margarine mixture, and the buttermilk and egg. Combine well, using your hands. Press the mixture into the prepared baking tin. Level the mixture and bake for 30 minutes, until slightly browned.

STEP FIVE Remove from the oven and reduce the temperature to 90°C/190°F/Gas ¼. Divide the baked mixture into 8 x 6 cm (3 x 2¼ in) bars, remove from the baking tin and divide the bars between two baking trays and bake for about 4 hours, until dry and crisp.

Makes 4 portions

ITALIAN RICE SALAD

PREP: 12 MINS
COOK: 10 MINS

175 g (6 oz) long-grain rice
1 bunch spring onions,
    thinly sliced
1 cooked skinless chicken
    breast, shredded
100 g (4 oz) pine nuts, toasted
    (see tip on page 104)
2 tomatoes, deseeded and
    chopped
2 tbsp chopped fresh
    parsley leaves
salt and black pepper

FOR THE DRESSING
5 tbsp olive oil
4 tbsp finely grated
    Parmesan cheese
½ garlic clove, crushed
2 tbsp white wine vinegar

Toasted pine nuts make a tasty, crunchy addition to this healthy Mediterranean salad. Either make your own dressing or use a shop-bought one.

STEP ONE Cook the rice in a saucepan of lightly salted boiling water according to the packet instructions, then drain and refresh under cold running water.

STEP TWO Put the drained rice, spring onions, shredded chicken, toasted pine nuts, chopped tomatoes and parsley into a mixing bowl. Season well.

STEP THREE Whisk the dressing ingredients together, then pour the dressing over the salad. Toss to combine before serving.

Makes 2 wraps

CHICKEN, AVOCADO AND TOMATO WRAPS

PREP: 12 MINS

2 mini tortilla wraps
1 cooked skinless chicken
    breast, diced
1 large tomato, deseeded
    and chopped
1 ripe avocado, halved, stoned,
    peeled and chopped
1 large spring onion, sliced
3 tbsp light mayonnaise
squeeze of lime juice
50 g (2 oz) Cheddar
    cheese, grated
salt and black pepper

Awaken your senses with these chicken and avocado wraps, pepped up with a hint of lime. They take seconds to make but taste so good.

STEP ONE Warm the tortilla wraps in the microwave for 20 seconds, or on each side in a dry frying pan, then place them on a board.

STEP TWO Mix the chicken, tomato, avocado, spring onion, mayonnaise and lime juice together in a bowl. Season to taste and spoon along one side of each wrap.

STEP THREE Sprinkle with the grated cheese, roll up, then slice each wrap into three pieces to serve.

Makes 2 wraps

HONEY CHICKEN AND HUMMUS WRAPS

PREP: 12 MINS
COOK: 5 MINS

1 large skinless chicken breast
1 tbsp runny honey
2 tbsp olive oil
2 mini tortilla wraps
2 tbsp hummus
1 carrot, grated
½ Little Gem lettuce, sliced
salt and black pepper

Hummus, carrot and honey make for an irresistible flavour combination. You can substitute the chicken with turkey, or for a vegetarian version replace the chicken with halloumi and add cucumber, avocado and tomato, instead of the hummus and carrot.

STEP ONE Put the chicken breast on a board, season and cover with clingfilm. Bash it with a rolling pin until thin, then remove the clingfilm and rub the honey into the chicken.

STEP TWO Heat the olive oil in a frying pan over a medium heat. Fry the chicken for about 5 minutes, turning it over halfway through, until cooked, then remove from the pan and leave to rest.

STEP THREE Warm the wraps in the microwave for 20 seconds, or on each side in a dry frying pan, then place them on a clean board.

STEP FOUR Spread half the hummus over one of the wraps and top with grated carrot and lettuce. Slice half of the honey chicken and arrange on top. Roll up, then slice the wrap in half to serve. Repeat with the second wrap and remaining filling ingredients.

Makes 4 wraps

BEEF, RED PEPPER AND PICKLED RED ONION WRAPS

PREP: 10 MINS
COOK: 5–6 MINS

2 x 200 g (7 oz) sirloin steaks
1 tbsp olive oil
½ red onion, thinly sliced
white wine vinegar
4 tortilla wraps or flatbreads
1 ripe avocado, halved,
   stoned and peeled
lime, halved, for squeezing
4 roasted red peppers (from
   a jar), thinly sliced
2 spring onions, thinly sliced
   or julienned
salt and black pepper

These are popular lunchtime wraps in our house. Make sure you add pickled red onion to give them that extra sweet-and-sour taste. The steak can be cooked the day before, or you could use leftover roast beef.

STEP ONE Heat a frying pan over a high heat. Rub the olive oil over the steaks and season. Fry the steaks for 2–3 minutes on each side, then remove from the pan and set aside to rest.

STEP TWO Meanwhile, place the sliced red onion in a bowl, cover with white wine vinegar and set aside. Once cool, cut the steak into thin slices.

STEP THREE Warm the wraps in the microwave for 20 seconds, or on each side in a dry frying pan, then place them on a board.

STEP FOUR Mash the avocado with a squeeze of lime juice, and spoon a little mashed avocado over each wrap. Arrange slices of steak, red onion, red pepper and spring onion on top. Roll up, slice in half to serve, then repeat with the remaining wraps and filling ingredients.

TIP
Rub the steaks with some Cajun seasoning before frying, and add chopped fresh red chillies to the wraps, if you like a little heat.

Makes 6 portions

BEEF NOODLE SALAD

PREP: 15 MINS
COOK: 10 MINS

150 g (5 oz) medium
  egg noodles
175 g (6 oz) broccoli florets
2 carrots, sliced into thin
  matchsticks
1 bunch spring onions, sliced
100 g (4 oz) bean sprouts
2 tbsp sunflower oil, for frying
2 x 175 g (6 oz) sirloin steaks
salt and black pepper

FOR THE DRESSING
1 red chilli, deseeded and diced
1 garlic clove, crushed
2 tbsp sunflower oil
2 tbsp soy sauce
2 tbsp mirin
1 tbsp runny honey
juice of 1 lime

This crunchy Asian-style salad tastes great and is packed with nutrients.

STEP ONE Cook the noodles in lightly salted boiling water according to the packet instructions, then drain and refresh under cold running water. Snip the noodles into short lengths.

STEP TWO Blanch the broccoli in a saucepan of boiling water for 3 minutes, drain and refresh in cold water. Put all of the vegetables and the bean sprouts into a large bowl. Add the cooked noodles and season to taste.

STEP THREE Heat the oil in a frying pan over a high heat. Season the steaks then fry for 2–3 minutes on each side until brown, but still pink in the middle. Remove and set aside to rest on a plate.

STEP FOUR Mix together the dressing ingredients and pour them over the salad. Toss together. Slice the steak into strips and gently mix into the noodle salad.

Makes 3 wraps

SPICY PRAWN WRAPS

PREP: 10 MINS

3 mini tortilla wraps
4 tbsp light mayonnaise
1 tbsp tomato ketchup
½ tsp horseradish sauce
dash of Tabasco sauce
    (to taste)
200 g (7 oz) small, cooked
    prawns
a few leaves of Little Gem
    lettuce, shredded
salt and black pepper

If you like your wraps extra spicy, add some more Tabasco sauce.

STEP ONE Warm the wraps in the microwave for 20 seconds, or on each side in a dry frying pan, then place them on a board.

STEP TWO Mix the mayonnaise, tomato ketchup, horseradish sauce, Tabasco sauce and prawns together and season to taste.

STEP THREE Arrange a little shredded lettuce on one side of each wrap. Top with prawn mixture and roll up. Slice each wrap into three pieces to serve.

Makes 8 bruschettas

THREE-TOMATO BRUSCHETTAS

PREP: 15 MINS
COOK: 6 MINS

200 g (7 oz) ripe plum
   tomatoes (about 5)
200 g (7 oz) cherry tomatoes,
   quartered
100 g (4 oz) sundried tomatoes
   in oil, drained and cut into
   fine strips
50 ml (2 fl oz) olive oil
2 tsp red wine vinegar
1 small bunch fresh basil
   leaves, shredded
8 slices ciabatta bread
1 garlic clove, halved
salt and black pepper

This dish uses three varieties of tomatoes, to give the topping a full, sweet flavour. Just load up the topping on the toasted bread – it's that simple.

STEP ONE Cut a cross in the base of the plum tomatoes and blanch them in boiling water for about 20 seconds. Remove and place immediately in a bowl of cold water. Once cooled, peel the tomatoes, cut into chunks, remove the seeds and place the chunks in a large bowl. Add the quartered cherry tomatoes and strips of sundried tomato.

STEP TWO Add the olive oil, red wine vinegar and basil to the tomatoes and stir. Season and set aside for 10 minutes.

STEP THREE Preheat the grill and toast the ciabatta slices for about 3 minutes on each side, until golden brown, then rub each slice with the garlic halves. Pile the tomatoes onto each bruschetta, along with the juices from the bowl, and serve immediately.

Makes 4 portions

ORZO AND PRAWN CONFETTI SALAD

PREP: 8 MINS
COOK: 12 MINS

200 g (7 oz) orzo
6 heaped tbsp light
   mayonnaise
3 tbsp tomato ketchup
a few drops Worcestershire
   sauce
1 tbsp lemon juice
2 tomatoes, deseeded
   and diced
1 bunch spring onions, sliced
198 g (7 oz) can sweetcorn,
   drained
200 g (7 oz) small,
   cooked prawns
salt and black pepper
Little Gem lettuce, leaves
   separated, to serve
lemon wedges, to serve

This delicious, vibrant rainbow salad uses orzo, a form of pasta shaped like a large grain of rice.

STEP ONE Cook the orzo in a saucepan of lightly salted boiling water according to the packet instructions. Drain and refresh under cold running water.

STEP TWO Place the mayonnaise, tomato ketchup and Worcestershire sauce in a large bowl. Add the lemon juice and whisk in 4 tablespoons of cold water until the dressing is smooth. Add the remaining ingredients, including the cooked orzo, and season to taste. Mix together to combine and serve on the crunchy lettuce leaves.

TIP
To get the maximum amount of juice from a lemon or lime, roll it firmly with the palm of your hand on the work surface for a minute before cutting and juicing.

CHEESE STRAWS WITH PESTO AND THYME

PREP: 25 MINS
COOK: 17 MINS

320 g (11 oz) packet ready-
    rolled puff pastry
a little plain flour, for dusting
2 tbsp fresh green pesto
50 g (2 oz) Parmesan cheese,
    finely grated
50 g (2 oz) mature Cheddar
    cheese, grated
1 tbsp chopped fresh
    thyme leaves

These are so easy and fun to make. If you like, wrap them in Parma ham just before serving.

STEP ONE Preheat the oven to 220°C/425°F/Gas 7 and line a baking tray with non-stick baking paper.

STEP TWO Roll out the pastry to a 35 cm (14 in) square on a lightly floured work surface.

STEP THREE Brush the pastry with the pesto, then sprinkle over the grated cheeses and chopped thyme. Fold the pastry in half, covering the herby pesto and cheese layer, then re-roll to a rectangle about 20 x 35 cm (8 x 14 in). Trim the edges, cut into 12 mm (½ in) strips, and twist each strip to make a curl. Place the curled pastry strips on the prepared baking tray.

STEP FOUR Bake for about 12 minutes, then turn the strips over and continue to bake for another 5 minutes, until golden and crisp all over. The cheese straws will keep well in an airtight container for a couple of days.

TIP
Grated cheese can be sealed in a plastic food bag and stored in the freezer.

Makes 4 portions

CURRIED POTATO SALAD WITH ROASTED PEPPERS

PREP: 20 MINS
COOK: 20 MINS

2 red peppers, halved
  and deseeded
750 g (1 lb 10 oz) baby
  new potatoes, scrubbed
6 tbsp mayonnaise
6 tbsp natural yogurt
1 tbsp mango chutney
1½ tsp mild curry powder
squeeze of lemon juice
salt and black pepper

If you like, you could add some diced cooked chicken to this salad, or save time by using roasted peppers from a jar instead of roasting your own.

STEP ONE Preheat the oven to 200°C/400°F/Gas 6.

STEP TWO Place the peppers cut side down on a baking tray. Roast for 20 minutes, until golden, then transfer the roasted peppers to a bowl. Cover with clingfilm, leave to cool, then remove the clingfilm and peel the skin off the pepper halves. Slice the peppers into strips.

STEP THREE Meanwhile, put the potatoes in a saucepan with lightly salted cold water. Bring to the boil and cook for about 15 minutes, until tender. Drain and slice any large potatoes in half. Leave to cool.

STEP FOUR Mix the mayonnaise, yogurt, chutney, curry powder and lemon juice together in a large bowl. Add the cold potatoes and peppers, and season.

MELON, CUCUMBER AND CHERRY TOMATO SALAD

PREP: 20 MINS

1 small watermelon,
   halved and deseeded
1 cucumber, peeled, deseeded
   and sliced into thick
   crescent- shaped chunks
150 g (5 oz) cherry tomatoes,
   halved
1 cantaloupe melon,
   halved and deseeded
1 honeydew melon,
   halved and deseeded

FOR THE DRESSING
4 tbsp rice wine vinegar
8 tbsp light olive oil
1 tsp caster sugar
1 small bunch fresh mint
   leaves, chopped, plus
   extra leaves to serve
salt

I make this with a pretty orange and green mix of cantaloupe and honeydew, and like to use a melon baller for the watermelon. Children will enjoy helping you make them!

STEP ONE Using a melon baller, scoop out the flesh of the watermelon and place the balls in a bowl with the cucumber and tomatoes. Cut up the remaining melon flesh into wedges and add to the bowl.

STEP TWO Combine all of the dressing ingredients, toss with the melon, cucumber and tomatoes, and season. Add the mint leaves, and serve.

MINI CHEESE AND TOMATO TARTLETS

**PREP: 25 MINS,
PLUS CHILLING
COOK: 15 MINS**

FOR THE PASTRY
175 g (6 oz) plain flour,
    plus extra for dusting
75 g (3 oz) chilled unsalted
    butter, cubed
1 large egg, beaten
salt and black pepper

FOR THE FILLING
1 tbsp olive oil
2 onions, finely chopped
1 tbsp chopped fresh
    thyme leaves
2 large eggs, beaten
150 ml (¼ pint) double cream
12 cherry tomatoes, halved
25 g (1 oz) Parmesan cheese,
    finely grated
salt and black pepper

This recipe is bound to incite some serious lunchbox envy. With melt-in-the-mouth pastry and the most delicious cheese, tomato, onion and thyme filling, these tartlets make a great lunch or mouthwatering canapé.

STEP ONE To make the pastry, put the flour and butter into the bowl of a food processor with a little seasoning. Whizz until the mixture resembles breadcrumbs. Add the egg and 1 tablespoon of water and whizz until the mixture forms a ball.

STEP TWO Roll out the pastry on a clean, lightly floured work surface to 5 mm (¼ in) thick, then cut into 24 rounds using a 5 cm (2 in) fluted round cutter. Line each hole of 2 x 12-hole deep mini bun tins with the pastry circles and prick the bases with a fork. Chill in the fridge.

STEP THREE Preheat the oven to 200°C/400°F/Gas 6.

STEP FOUR To make the filling, heat the olive oil in a saucepan over a low heat. Add the onion and sauté for 5 minutes until soft. Add the thyme leaves, season to taste and leave to cool. Whisk the eggs and cream together in a jug.

STEP FIVE Remove the pastry from the fridge and divide the cooked onion evenly between the pastry cases. Top each with a cherry tomato half, cut side up. Pour over the egg and cream mixture and sprinkle the Parmesan cheese over the tarts. Bake the tarts for about 15 minutes, until golden on top and crisp underneath.

Chapter five

STORECUPBOARD

PENNE ALL'ARRABBIATA

PREP: 15 MINS
COOK: 20 MINS

300 g (11 oz) penne
4 tbsp olive oil
2 red onions, finely chopped
1 red chilli, deseeded and diced
2–3 garlic cloves, crushed
2 x 400 g (14 oz) cans
    chopped tomatoes
2 tsp caster sugar
1 tbsp tomato purée
2 tsp balsamic vinegar
2 bay leaves
2 tbsp chopped fresh
    basil leaves
salt and black pepper

I like to add a touch of chilli to my tomato sauce, to give it a bit of a kick.

STEP ONE Cook the pasta in a large saucepan of lightly salted boiling water according to the packet instructions, retaining 2 tablespoons of the cooking water before draining.

STEP TWO Meanwhile, heat 2 tablespoons of the olive oil in a saucepan over a medium heat. Add the onion, chilli and garlic and fry for 5 minutes until just soft, then add the tomatoes, sugar, tomato purée, balsamic vinegar and bay leaves. Bring to the boil then simmer, uncovered, for 15 minutes until reduced.

STEP THREE Remove the bay leaves, stir in the chopped basil, and add the cooked pasta and reserved water to the sauce with the remaining olive oil. Season and toss together.

TIPS
If you don't have fresh chillies to hand, use a pinch of dried chilli flakes instead. Canned whole plum tomatoes work just as well as chopped – just squish them against the side of the pan to break them up as you simmer the sauce.

*Makes 4–6 portions
(freezer friendly)*

CARROT AND CORIANDER SOUP

PREP: 15 MINS
COOK: 25 MINS

a knob of butter
1 onion, sliced
2 celery sticks, sliced
450 g (1 lb) carrots, sliced
1½ tsp ground coriander
1 tbsp plain flour
500 ml (7 fl oz) vegetable stock
2 tbsp crème fraîche
salt and black pepper
fresh coriander leaves,
    to garnish

Carrots are rich in antioxidants, particularly beta-carotene, and interestingly they have an even higher concentration of antioxidants when they are cooked.

STEP ONE Melt the butter in a large, deep saucepan. Add the onion, celery and carrots and sauté for 2 minutes until soft. Add the ground coriander and flour, stir for a minute, then gradually stir in the stock. Cover, bring to the boil, then reduce the heat and simmer for 15 minutes until the vegetables are tender.

STEP TWO Blend the soup until smooth, using an electric hand blender. Season to taste, then add the crème fraîche and garnish with coriander leaves to serve.

**PREP: 10 MINS
COOK: 40 MINS**

2 tbsp olive oil
2 onions, chopped
2 garlic cloves, crushed
75 g (3 oz) dried green lentils
1 litre (1¾ pints) strong
   vegetable stock
150 g (5 oz) frozen peas
200 g (7 oz) fresh spinach
50 ml (2 fl oz) double cream
salt and black pepper

TASTY SPINACH SOUP

A healthy soup that is vibrant in colour and taste, and packed with superfood goodness from the earthy spinach and lentils.

STEP ONE Heat the olive oil in a large, deep saucepan over a medium heat and sauté the onions and garlic for 3 minutes. Stir in the lentils, then add the stock. Bring to the boil, then cover and simmer for 30 minutes, until the lentils are tender.

STEP TWO Add the peas and spinach and cook for a further 3–4 minutes, then blend the soup until smooth, using an electric hand blender. Season to taste and stir in the cream before serving.

Makes 20 vegetable bites (freezer friendly)

PREP: 20 MINS
COOK: 12 MINS

2 slices stale white bread
400 g (14 oz) can chickpeas,
    drained and rinsed
2 tsp ground cumin
2 tsp ground coriander
1 onion, chopped
1 carrot, grated
25 g (1 oz) Parmesan
    cheese, grated
2 garlic cloves, crushed
1 tbsp chopped fresh
    parsley leaves
1 small egg, lightly beaten
a little sunflower oil, for frying
a little plain flour, for dusting
salt and black pepper

FOR THE QUICK TZATZIKI
250 g (9 oz) natural
    Greek yogurt
½ cucumber, grated
1 garlic clove, grated

TO SERVE
mayonnaise or yogurt
toasted pitta breads
lime wedges
mint leaves

FALAFEL-STYLE VEGETABLE BITES

Shop-bought falafel can sometimes be quite dry, but these are deliciously moist. They're simple to make, too – you just blitz all the ingredients together.

STEP ONE Make the quick tzatziki by combining all the ingredients in a bowl. Cover and chill in the fridge.

STEP TWO Put the bread into the bowl of a food processor and whizz until they resemble fine breadcrumbs. Add the drained chickpeas, spices, onion, carrot, cheese, garlic and parsley. Whizz until finely chopped, then season. Add the egg, a little at a time, and pulse until combined (you may not need all the egg).

STEP THREE Remove the bowl from the processor and, using your hands, shape the falafel mixture into 20 small patties. Dust them lightly with flour.

STEP FOUR Heat a little sunflower oil in a frying pan over a medium heat. Fry the patties in batches for 2–3 minutes on each side, until golden and crisp. Drain on kitchen paper before serving with mayonnaise or yogurt, toasted pitta breads, lime wedges for squeezing, and a green salad.

FRITTATA WITH CHERRY TOMATOES

PREP: 12 MINS
COOK: 18–20 MINS

2 tbsp olive oil
2 small onions, thinly sliced
8 cooked new potatoes,
    scrubbed and thickly sliced
30 g (1¼ oz) mature Cheddar
    cheese, grated
5 medium eggs, beaten
2 tbsp whole milk
8 cherry tomatoes, halved
1 tbsp snipped chives
salt and black pepper

This is probably my favourite combination of flavours for a frittata, and it makes a great easy lunch or supper dish. Squirrel away a wedge for your child's lunchbox next day, too... it's guaranteed not to be returned to sender. Serve with salad on the side.

STEP ONE Preheat the grill to medium-high.

STEP TWO Heat the olive oil in a 18–20 cm (7–8 in) small non-stick omelette pan over a low heat. Add the onion and sauté for about 5 minutes until soft. Add the potatoes, stir and season to taste.

STEP THREE In a bowl, add the grated cheese to the eggs and milk, then season and pour into the omelette pan. Cook gently over a medium heat until set around the edges, then loosen the edges of the frittata with a spatula. Arrange the tomatoes, cut side up, on top of the frittata and sprinkle with chives.

STEP FOUR Place under the grill for about 5 minutes, until lightly golden and set in the middle. Slice into wedges, to serve hot or cold.

Makes 4–6 portions (freezer friendly)

RED LENTIL DAHL

PREP: 20 MINS
COOK: 20–25 MINS

2 tbsp sunflower oil
2 onions, chopped
2 carrots, diced
1 red pepper, deseeded
   and diced
1 tsp mild curry powder
1 tsp ground cumin
1 tsp ground coriander
½ tsp ground cinnamon
2 garlic cloves, crushed
2 cm (¾ in) piece of fresh root
   ginger, peeled and grated
200 g (7 oz) dried red lentils
400 g (14 oz) can chopped
   tomatoes
600 ml (1 pint) vegetable stock
juice of ½ small lemon
salt and black pepper

This nutritious dish is bursting with aromatic flavours. Serve with fluffy rice, or as a vegetarian option alongside other curries.

STEP ONE Heat the sunflower oil in a large saucepan over a medium heat, add the onions, carrots and red pepper and sauté for 3–4 minutes, until starting to soften. Add the spices, garlic and ginger and fry for 30 seconds.

STEP TWO Add the lentils, tomatoes and stock, bring to the boil, cover and simmer gently for 15–20 minutes, stirring from time to time, until the lentils are tender.

STEP THREE Stir in the lemon juice and season well before serving.

Makes 4 portions

SPAGHETTI WITH TOMATOES, PESTO AND CIABATTA CRUMBS

PREP: 8 MINS
COOK: 12 MINS

250 g (9 oz) spaghetti
3 tbsp olive oil
1 onion, chopped
2 garlic cloves, crushed
400 g (14 oz) can chopped
    tomatoes
3 tbsp fresh green pesto
25 g (1 oz) Parmesan
    cheese, grated
50 g (2 oz) ciabatta,
    cut into cubes
salt and black pepper

Add a twist to spaghetti with tomato sauce by adding vibrant pesto and some crunchy ciabatta croutons.

STEP ONE Cook the spaghetti in a large saucepan of lightly salted boiling water according to the packet instructions, then drain.

STEP TWO Meanwhile, heat 2 tablespoons of the olive oil in a frying pan. Add the onion and sauté for 3–4 minutes until soft, then add the garlic and sauté for a further minute. Add the tomatoes to the onions and garlic and simmer for 5 minutes. Add the pesto, then the cooked pasta and Parmesan. Toss together, season and transfer to warm bowls or plates.

STEP THREE Heat the remaining oil in the frying pan. Whizz the ciabatta cubes in a food processor until they form coarse crumbs, then add them to the pan and fry until crisp. Sprinkle on top of the pasta and serve immediately.

Makes 4 portions

QUINOA AND EDAMAME SALAD WITH HONEY AND GINGER DRESSING

PREP: 15 MINS
COOK: 4 MINS

150 g (5 oz) quinoa
1 carrot, grated
1 bunch spring onions,
    thinly sliced
4 tbsp canned sweetcorn
    kernels
100 g (4 oz) shelled edamame
    beans, cooked and refreshed
    under cold running water
salt and black pepper

FOR THE DRESSING
2 tbsp rice wine vinegar
4 tbsp olive oil
1 tsp runny honey
½ tsp grated fresh root ginger

For anyone who struggles to pronounce quinoa, it sounds like 'keen–wah'. It's one of the world's most popular superfoods, loaded with protein, fibre and minerals (and it doesn't contain gluten). Combine it with my tasty dressing and edamame (young soya) beans and you can have a super-healthy salad without compromising on taste.

STEP ONE Put the quinoa and 300 ml (½ pint) of water into a small saucepan. Cover, then bring to the boil. Stir and turn off the heat, then re-cover and set aside until all of the water has been absorbed. Season and leave to cool.

STEP TWO Place the cooked quinoa in a large bowl with the grated carrot, spring onions, sweetcorn and edamame beans.

STEP THREE Combine all of the dressing ingredients in a small bowl, then add to the salad and mix well before serving.

TIP
If your honey has solidified, spoon it into a microwave-safe bowl, pop it in the microwave for a few seconds and it will turn back into runny honey.

Makes 4–6 portions (freezer friendly)

INDIAN-SPICED CHICKEN WITH RICE

PREP: 15 MINS
COOK: 15 MINS

225 g (8 oz) long-grain
    or basmati rice
75 g (3 oz) frozen peas
2 tbsp olive oil
2 skinless chicken breasts,
    sliced into strips
1 large onion, chopped
1 tsp grated fresh root ginger
½ tsp garam masala
¼ tsp turmeric
1 tsp mild curry paste
25 g (1 oz) butter
1 tbsp mango chutney
30 g (1¼ oz) unsalted
    peanuts (optional)
2 tomatoes, deseeded
    and thinly sliced
salt and black pepper

Liven up chicken with an Indian-spiced coating. If you like it spicy, just add more curry paste. You can swap the chicken breasts for boneless chicken thighs or turkey breast, if you prefer.

STEP ONE Cook the rice in lightly salted boiling water according to the packet instructions, until tender. Add the peas to the rice 5 minutes before the end of the cooking time. Drain the rice and peas, and refresh under cold water.

STEP TWO Heat the oil in a frying pan over a high heat. Season the chicken strips, then fry until browned and cooked through. Transfer to a plate.

STEP THREE Add the onion and ginger to the frying pan and sauté for 5 minutes until soft. Add the spices and curry paste and fry for 30 seconds, then add the butter, mango chutney and chicken strips. Stir together until the butter has melted. Add the rice and peas and toss together over the heat until hot. Garnish with the peanuts, if using, and tomatoes.

Makes 4 portions

SAUSAGES WITH CHEESY MASH AND ONION GRAVY

PREP: 20 MINS
COOK: 20–25 MINS

8 Cumberland sausages
(or sausages of your choice)

FOR THE MASHED
POTATOES
750 g (1 lb 10 oz) floury
potatoes, peeled and
cut into chunks
200 g (7 oz) carrots, sliced
a knob of butter
125 ml (4 fl oz) whole milk
50 g (2 oz) Gruyère
cheese, grated
salt and black pepper

FOR THE GRAVY
a knob of butter
1 onion, thinly sliced
1 garlic clove, crushed
¼ tsp Spanish sweet
smoked paprika
1 tsp tomato purée
450 ml (¾ pint) beef stock
2 tsp Worcestershire sauce
1 tsp soy sauce
1 tbsp cornflour

Try my twist on classic sausage and mash: adding Gruyère cheese to the potatoes and covering the sausages with onion gravy makes all the difference. You won't look back!

STEP ONE Preheat the oven to 200°C/400°F/Gas 6.

STEP TWO Place the sausages on a baking tray and roast in the oven for 20–25 minutes until golden brown and cooked through.

STEP THREE Meanwhile, boil the potatoes in lightly salted boiling water for 15–20 minutes, until tender, then drain. In a separate pan, boil the carrots for 15–20 minutes, until tender. Return the cooked potatoes to the empty saucepan and mash with the butter, milk and Gruyère cheese until smooth.

STEP FOUR Drain the carrots, then blend until smooth using an electric hand blender. Stir the carrot purée into the mashed potatoes.

STEP FIVE To make the gravy, heat the butter in a saucepan over a medium heat, then add the onion and garlic and sauté until lightly golden and soft. Add the paprika and tomato purée, then stir in the stock, Worcestershire sauce and soy sauce. Bring to the boil. Blend the cornflour with 1 tablespoon of water, then add it to the pan, stir until thickened and serve with the sausages and mashed potato.

Makes 4 portions

SAUSAGE AND BEAN HOTPOT

PREP: 8 MINS
COOK: 25–30 MINS

4 sausages
1 tbsp olive oil
1 onion, chopped
1 carrot, diced
1 garlic clove, crushed
400 g (14 oz) can chopped
    tomatoes
200 g (7 oz) can cannellini
    beans, drained and rinsed
1 tsp tomato purée
1 tsp chopped fresh
    thyme leaves
150 g (5 oz) potato,
    peeled and diced
50 g (2 oz) Cheddar
    cheese, grated
salt and black pepper

A simple recipe that makes the most of lots of classic ingredients. If you fancy, substitute diced skinless chicken thighs for the sausages, and add them with the cannellini beans.

STEP ONE Preheat the oven to 180°C/350°F/Gas 4. Place the sausages on a baking tray and roast in the oven for 20–25 minutes, until golden brown and cooked through.

STEP TWO Meanwhile, heat the olive oil in a saucepan over a medium heat. Add the onion and carrot and sauté for 5 minutes. Add the garlic and sauté for a further minute, then add the tomatoes, beans, tomato purée and thyme. Cover and simmer for 10 minutes.

STEP THREE Slice each sausage into six, then add the sausage chunks to the pan. Season and spoon the hotpot into a shallow, heatproof serving dish.

STEP FOUR Meanwhile, cook the diced potato in lightly salted boiling water for 5–7 minutes, until tender, then drain and scatter on top of the sausage and beans.

STEP FIVE Sprinkle with the cheese and pop under a hot grill for 5 minutes until bubbling, before serving.

> **TIP**
> If you want to save herbs while they are still fresh,
> finely chop them and freeze in ice cube trays.
> You will then have fresh herbs ready to throw
> into soups, casseroles or stews whenever you want.

Makes 4 portions

POACHED EGGS WITH RED ONION, TOMATO AND PEPPER RAGÙ

PREP: 6 MIN
COOK: 20 MINS

2 tbsp olive oil
½ large red onion, sliced
1 small red pepper,
    deseeded and diced
1 garlic clove, crushed
400 g (14 oz) can
    chopped tomatoes
1 tbsp tomato purée
pinch of caster sugar
4 large eggs
salt and black pepper

This is my version of a popular South American breakfast, and it's as good for breakfast as it is for lunch, served with a hunk of crusty bread to mop up all the delicious sauce.

STEP ONE Heat the olive oil in a small lidded frying or omelette pan. Add the onion and red pepper and sauté for 5 minutes until just soft. Season and add the garlic. Fry for 30 seconds, then add the tomatoes, tomato purée and sugar. Cover and simmer for 8–10 minutes until the sauce has reduced.

STEP TWO Make four holes in the mixture in the pan. Crack an egg into each hole and season. Cover and gently poach for about 5 minutes until the egg whites have set.

Makes 4 portions

PENNE WITH ROASTED BUTTERNUT SQUASH AND BACON

PREP: 15 MINS
COOK: 15–20 MINS

300 g (11 oz) butternut
squash, peeled, deseeded
and cubed
200 g (7 oz) smoked bacon
lardons, chopped
2 tbsp olive oil
1 tsp chopped fresh
thyme leaves
300 g (11 oz) penne
20 g (¾ oz) butter
20 g (¾ oz) plain flour
450 ml (¾ pint) whole milk
30 g (1¼ oz) Parmesan
cheese, grated
salt and black pepper
fresh flat-leaf parsley leaves,
chopped, to garnish

To make a vegetarian version of this simple pasta dish, leave out the bacon lardons and add 75 g (3 oz) frozen peas to the pasta water for the last 3–4 minutes of cooking time.

STEP ONE Preheat the oven to 200°C/400°F/Gas 6 and line a baking tray with non-stick baking paper.

STEP TWO Arrange the squash and bacon on the prepared baking tray. Season, drizzle the squash with the olive oil and sprinkle over the thyme. Roast for 10–15 minutes, until golden and crispy. Remove from the oven and set aside.

STEP THREE Meanwhile, cook the pasta in a large saucepan of lightly salted boiling water according to the packet instructions, then drain.

STEP FOUR To make the sauce, melt the butter in a saucepan over a medium heat. Add the flour and stir over the heat for 1 minute. Gradually whisk in the milk, stirring constantly until thickened. Season and add the Parmesan cheese, then add the bacon, squash and drained pasta and gently mix together. Sprinkle with chopped parsley to serve.

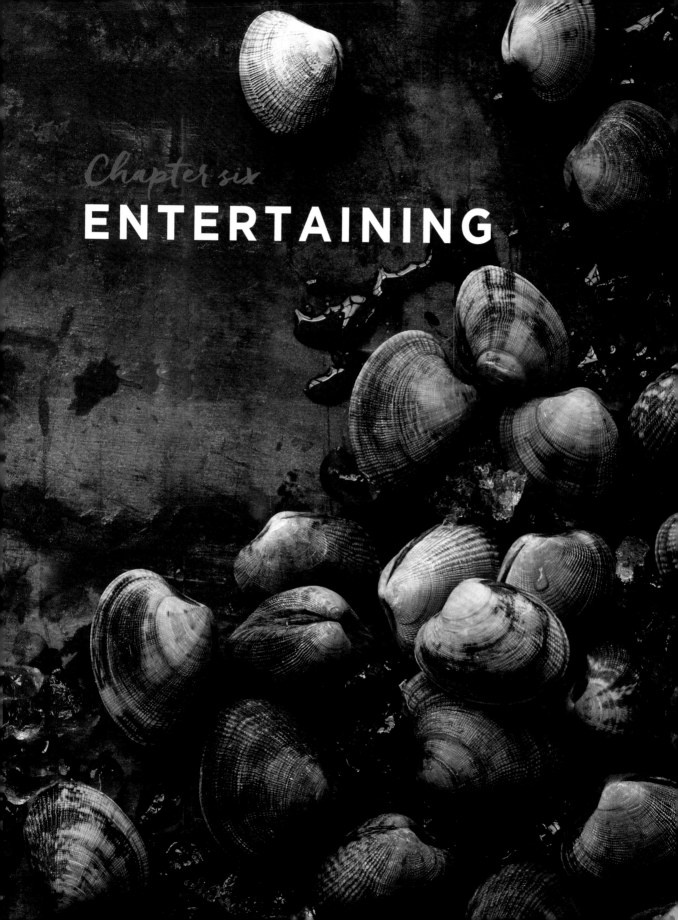

Chapter six
ENTERTAINING

BAKED TOMATO RISOTTO

PREP: 20 MINS
COOK: 25 MINS

2 tbsp olive oil
2 onions, finely diced
2 garlic cloves, crushed
225 g (8 oz) risotto rice
150 ml (¼ pint) white wine
750 ml (1¼ pints) vegetable
   or chicken stock
50 g (2 oz) sundried tomatoes
   (in oil), chopped
150 g (5 oz) cherry tomatoes,
   halved
75 g (3 oz) Parmesan
   cheese, grated
2 ripe tomatoes, deseeded
   and diced
2 tbsp chopped fresh
   basil leaves
salt and black pepper

The traditional method for making risotto involves adding liquid gradually, and requires you to stand over the hob while it cooks. With this oven-baked version, you can catch up on emails or put your feet up with a glass of wine instead (there is always some left over from making the risotto), and you still get a perfect result.

STEP ONE Preheat the oven to 160°C/325°F/Gas 3.

STEP TWO Heat the olive oil in an ovenproof, lidded saucepan. Add the onions and garlic and sauté for 3–4 minutes until soft. Add the rice and stir to make sure that it is well coated. Add the white wine, stock and sundried tomatoes. Bring to the boil. Cover with the lid and transfer to the oven to cook for 15 minutes.

STEP THREE Put the cherry tomato halves on a baking tray and drizzle over 1 tablespoon of oil from the jar of sundried tomatoes. Bake in the oven for 15 minutes while the risotto is cooking, then remove from the oven, transfer to a bowl or jug and blend until smooth using an electric hand blender.

STEP FOUR Remove the risotto from the oven (the rice should still have a slight bite). Stir in the puréed cherry tomatoes, grated Parmesan and diced tomatoes. Season to taste and stir in the basil.

*Makes 6 portions
(freezer friendly)*

CHICKEN IN A CREAMY MUSHROOM SAUCE

PREP: 15 MINS
COOK: 35 MINS

30 g (1¼ oz) butter
2 tbsp olive oil
6 chicken breasts (skin on)
2 onions, chopped
2 garlic cloves, crushed
30 g (1¼ oz) plain flour
200 ml (7 fl oz) white wine
200 ml (7 fl oz) chicken stock
1 tbsp chopped fresh
    thyme leaves
300 g (11 oz) button
    mushrooms, sliced
200 ml (7 fl oz) double cream
squeeze of lemon juice
salt and black pepper

Give this French-inspired dish a go, making sure you cook the chicken gently, so that it remains tender. Serve with fluffy white rice.

STEP ONE Heat the butter with the oil in a large, lidded frying pan and brown the chicken, skin side down, for a few minutes, in batches if necessary, then set aside. Add the onion and garlic and sauté until just soft. Add the flour and stir for 1 minute. Pour in the wine and stock, bring to a simmer and stir until thickened.

STEP TWO Return the chicken to the pan with the thyme, cover and simmer gently for about 15 minutes until the chicken is cooked through.

STEP THREE Remove the chicken from the pan and set aside, then add the mushrooms and cook for 3 minutes. Add the cream and simmer for 3–5 minutes, until the sauce reduces to a coating consistency. Return the chicken to the pan and season to taste.

TIP
Button mushrooms are more than adequate here in this dish, but earthy Portobello and other large, open-cup varieties such as chestnut mushrooms are wonderful, too, and have a slightly stronger taste.

Makes 4 portions

BALSAMIC CHICKEN WITH WHITE WINE

PREP: 12 MINS
COOK: 50 MINS

2 tbsp olive oil
50 g (2 oz) butter
4 chicken thighs (skin on,
　and boneless if possible)
2 chicken breasts (skin on)
1 onion, finely chopped
2 garlic cloves, crushed
1 tbsp chopped fresh
　thyme leaves
150 ml (¼ pint) white wine
150 ml (¼ pint) chicken stock
1 tbsp balsamic vinegar
　(or to taste)
salt and black pepper

It's really worthwhile buying good-quality balsamic vinegar, as it tends to be sweeter and have a better depth of flavour. Serve with rice or roasted new potatoes (see page 55).

STEP ONE Heat the oil and butter in a large, lidded frying pan over a medium heat. Add the chicken thighs and breasts, skin side down, and fry on both sides until golden brown, then set aside.

STEP TWO Add the onion, garlic and thyme to the pan and sauté for 2 minutes. Add the white wine and stock, and return the chicken, skin side up, to the pan. Cover and simmer for about 40 minutes.

STEP THREE When the chicken is cooked through – the breasts may well be cooked after 15 minutes – transfer to a warm plate. The thighs may take longer to cook than the chicken breasts if they are on the bone. Remove the lid and raise the heat to reduce the liquid by half, season to taste and add the balsamic vinegar. Pour the sauce over the chicken to serve.

TIP
When chopping herbs, toss a little salt onto the chopping board; it will keep the herbs from flying around.

Makes 4 portions

WILD MUSHROOM GRATIN

PREP: 12 MINS
COOK: 15 MINS

2 tbsp olive oil
30 g (1¼ oz) butter
1 garlic clove, crushed
250 g (9 oz) chestnut
   mushrooms, halved
250 g (9 oz) small Portobello
   mushrooms, thickly sliced
250 g (9 oz) mixed wild
   mushrooms, thickly sliced
75 g (3 oz) Parmesan
   cheese, grated
salt and black pepper

You can buy a wonderful variety of mushrooms in supermarkets now (see overleaf), and this is a simple but delicious and elegant way to serve them.

STEP ONE Preheat the grill until very hot.

STEP TWO Heat a frying pan or wok over a high heat. Add the olive oil and half of the butter. When the butter has melted, add half of the garlic with the chestnut and Portobello mushrooms. Sauté for 2 minutes, until they are just turning brown, then spoon into a shallow, ovenproof dish.

STEP THREE Repeat with the remaining butter and garlic and the wild mushrooms. Scatter the wild mushrooms on top of the mushrooms in the dish. Season and sprinkle with the Parmesan cheese.

STEP FOUR Grill for 5 minutes, or until the cheese has melted and the mushrooms are lightly browned. Serve immediately.

VENISON CASSEROLE

PREP: 20 MINS
COOK: 2 HOURS 15 MINS

2 tbsp olive oil
1 kg (2¼ lb) venison
    stewing steak, cut into
    bite-sized pieces
a knob of butter
2 leeks, trimmed and sliced
2 celery sticks, sliced
40 g (1½ oz) plain flour
150 ml (¼ pint) port
400 ml (13 fl oz) beef stock
2 tbsp orange juice
200 g (7 oz) baby carrots
1 tbsp Worcestershire sauce
1 tbsp chopped fresh
    thyme leaves
1 tsp soft light brown sugar
salt and black pepper

Long, slow cooking brings the best out of lean cuts, making them sweet and tender and giving all the flavours time to come together. If you prefer, you could also make this with beef. Serve with mashed potatoes.

STEP ONE Preheat the oven to 130°C/260°F/Gas ½.

STEP TWO Heat the oil in a deep, heavy-based, lidded casserole over a high heat, then brown the venison, in batches if necessary, until browned all over. Remove from the casserole and set aside.

STEP THREE Melt the butter in the casserole, add the leeks and celery and sauté over a medium heat for 5 minutes, until soft. Sprinkle the flour over the vegetables, stir for a minute, then add the port and beef stock. Bring to the boil, then add the remaining ingredients and the browned venison.

STEP FOUR Season, cover and transfer to the oven to cook for about 2 hours, until the venison meat is tender.

TIP
Don't overcrowd your casserole, pan or roasting tin when browning or roasting meat or vegetables. If you cram too much in the pan, instead of cooking in batches, the temperature decreases and they steam, so you won't get the lovely caramelisation.

Makes 4–6 portions

ORIENTAL ROAST DUCK WITH CHINESE-STYLE RICE

PREP: 15 MINS, PLUS MARINATING COOK: 1 HOUR

2 tbsp hoisin sauce
2 tbsp soy sauce
2 tbsp sweet chilli sauce
1 kg (2¼ lb) crown of duck, skin scored

FOR THE CHINESE-STYLE RICE
250 g (9 oz) long-grain rice
2 carrots, diced
50 g (2 oz) frozen peas
2 tbsp sunflower oil
2 onions, diced
1 tsp grated fresh root ginger
200 g (7 oz) baby corn, sliced into rounds
200 g (7 oz) button mushrooms, sliced
2 tbsp soy sauce
1 tbsp hoisin sauce
salt and black pepper

Marinating the duck in a mix of hoisin, soy and chilli sauce gives it a wonderful flavour, and served with my delicious Chinese-style rice, it makes for a show-stopping meal.

STEP ONE Place the hoisin sauce, soy sauce and sweet chilli sauce into a large bowl and add the duck crown, smothering it in the marinade ingredients before covering and leaving to marinate in the fridge for an hour.

STEP TWO Preheat the oven to 200°C/400°F/Gas 6, line a roasting tin with foil and place a grill rack on top of the foil.

STEP THREE Remove the duck from the marinade and put it, crown side down, onto the rack. Roast for 30 minutes until brown, then turn over and roast for a further 30–35 minutes, until golden brown and cooked through. Remove from the oven and leave to rest, covered in foil.

STEP FOUR Meanwhile, cook the rice with the diced carrots in lightly salted boiling water for 12–15 minutes, until the carrots are tender. Add the peas 5 minutes before the end of the cooking time, then drain.

STEP FIVE Heat the sunflower oil in a wok or frying pan over a medium heat. Add the onion and ginger and stir-fry for 5 minutes, then add the baby corn and mushrooms and stir-fry for a further 3 minutes. Add the cooked rice and carrots and toss over the heat for a couple of minutes to warm through. Mix the soy sauce and hoisin sauce together in a bowl, then add to the rice, stir and season well. Serve with the roasted duck.

Makes 6 portions

SLOW-ROAST SHOULDER OF LAMB WITH POTATOES AND LEEKS

PREP: 20 MINS
COOK: ABOUT 4 HOURS

3 leeks, trimmed and
    thinly sliced
5 medium potatoes, peeled
    and sliced into 4–6 wedges
½ bunch fresh thyme sprigs
900 ml (1½ pints) chicken
    stock
1 large shoulder of lamb
1 garlic clove, crushed
1 tbsp runny honey
salt and black pepper

Shoulder of lamb is one of the cheaper cuts of lamb, but also one of the most delicious. The long, slow cooking renders the meat so tender and juicy, it just falls off the bone. The meat is also delicious served cold the next day.

STEP ONE Preheat the oven to 200°C/400°F/Gas 6.

STEP TWO Put the leeks, potatoes and half the thyme sprigs into a roasting tin. Pour over the chicken stock, and roughly chop the remaining thyme leaves. Place a grill rack over the vegetables.

STEP THREE Season the lamb shoulder and place it on the grill rack, then scatter the chopped thyme leaves over the meat, rub in the crushed garlic and drizzle honey over the top.

STEP FOUR Roast the lamb for 30 minutes, until brown, then turn the oven temperature down to 130°C/250°F/Gas ½ and roast it for a further 3–4 hours, until tender, basting the lamb with the cooking juices from time to time. Serve the lamb with the vegetables, and spoon over any remaining cooking juices.

TIP
To save yourself time, keep a bowl next to you while you're prepping, for throwing peelings and vegetable scraps, so you don't have to keep making trips to the bin or composter.

BEEF IN RED WINE SAUCE

PREP: 15 MINS
COOK: 15 MINS

3 tbsp sunflower oil
400 g (14 oz) fillet or sirloin
   steak, cut into thick strips
2 large banana shallots, sliced
1 garlic clove, crushed
150 g (5 oz) button
   mushrooms, sliced
1 tbsp plain flour
200 ml (7 fl oz) red wine
150 ml (¼ pint) beef stock
a pinch of caster sugar
1 tbsp chopped fresh
   thyme leaves
salt and black pepper

Thick strips of beef, simmered in a delicious pot of red wine sauce, make this dish an impressive, speedy take on beef stew. Serve with rice or mash, and steamed spinach.

STEP ONE Heat 2 tablespoons of the sunflower oil in a frying pan over a high heat. Season the beef strips and fry for a minute, in batches if necessary, until browned all over. Remove the beef and set aside.

STEP TWO Heat the remaining oil in the pan. Add the shallots, garlic and mushrooms and sauté for 3 minutes. Sprinkle over the flour, stir for a minute, then add the red wine and stock. Bring to the boil and simmer for 3–5 minutes, stirring, until reduced by half and thickened.

STEP THREE Add the sugar and thyme, return the beef to the pan, and simmer for 2 minutes.

STUFFED PEPPERS WITH RICE AND CHICKEN

PREP: 20 MINS
COOK: 25 MINS

3 large peppers (a combination
    of colours), sliced in half
    lengthways through the
    stalk and deseeded
1 tbsp olive oil, plus extra
    for drizzling
1 onion, chopped
1 garlic clove, crushed
175 g (6 oz) cooked chicken
    breast, diced
200 g (7 oz) cooked
    long-grain rice
2 tbsp chopped fresh
    basil leaves
75 g (3 oz) Gruyère
    cheese, grated
salt and black pepper

FOR THE TOMATO SAUCE
(OR USE A READY-MADE
TOMATO SAUCE)
200 ml (7 fl oz) tomato passata
2 tbsp sundried tomato paste
2 tbsp chopped fresh
    basil leaves

Brighten up the dinner table with multi-coloured stuffed peppers. With a tasty chicken filling, topped with tomato sauce and a sprinkle of bubbling melted cheese, these make a great starter for a dinner party as you can make them ahead of time and just heat them through before serving. Substitute vegetables like cooked diced carrot and courgette for the chicken if any of your guests are vegetarian.

STEP ONE Preheat the oven to 220°C/425°F/Gas 7.

STEP TWO Arrange the peppers, cut side up, in a roasting tin. Season, and drizzle over a little olive oil. Roast in the oven for 15 minutes until just soft. Remove from the oven and set aside.

STEP THREE Meanwhile, make the filling. Heat the olive oil in a frying pan over a medium heat. Add the onion and garlic and sauté until soft, then add the cooked chicken and rice, and sauté for a further 2 minutes. Add the basil and 50 g (2 oz) of the Gruyère cheese. Season, then divide the filling between the pepper halves.

STEP FOUR For the tomato sauce, mix the passata, sundried tomato paste and basil together. Put the stuffed peppers in a small ovenproof dish. Spoon over the sauce and sprinkle with the remaining cheese. Bake in the oven for 10 minutes, until golden.

TIP
Fresh basil keeps better at room temperature with the stems in water.

Makes 6 portions

ONE-POT CHICKEN WITH SPRING VEGETABLES

PREP: 20 MINS
COOK: 1 HOUR 20 MINS

1.5–1.6 kg (3¼ –3½ lb) chicken
3 tbsp olive oil
1 tsp runny honey
1 tsp lemon juice
300 g (11 oz) baby new
   potatoes, scrubbed and
   any larger ones halved
1 onion, thinly sliced
2 garlic cloves, peeled
   but left whole
200 g (7 oz) baby carrots
300 ml (½ pint) hot
   chicken stock
300 ml (½ pint) white wine
100 g (4 oz) frozen peas
2 tbsp fresh tarragon leaves
salt and black pepper

This tasty all-in-one meal not only saves on washing up, it's also a nourishing feast that brings together the fresh taste of spring with the intense savoury hit of roast chicken.

STEP ONE Preheat the oven to 200°C/400°F/Gas 6.

STEP TWO Put the chicken into a large, shallow ovenproof dish or skillet. Drizzle over the olive oil, honey and lemon juice and season. Roast for 30 minutes until lightly golden brown, then add the potatoes, onion, garlic and carrots and toss to coat with the olive oil, honey and lemon in the dish around the chicken.

STEP THREE Pour the stock and wine over the vegetables, then put the dish back in the oven for a further 45 minutes, until the chicken is golden brown and cooked through and the vegetables are tender (you might need to cover the chicken with foil if it is getting too brown). Add the peas and cook for a final 5 minutes.

STEP FOUR Remove from the oven and sprinkle with tarragon before serving.

Makes 2 portions

POACHED SEA BREAM WITH BABY NEW POTATOES

PREP: 20 MINS
COOK: 24–27 MINS

a knob of butter
1 onion, sliced
150 g (5 oz) baby new potatoes,
    scrubbed and thinly sliced
1 garlic clove, crushed
75 ml (3 fl oz) white wine
1 tsp plain flour
400 ml (13 fl oz) chicken
    or vegetable stock
1 tsp chopped fresh
    thyme leaves
2 sea bream fillets (skin on)
1 ripe tomato, deseeded
    and diced
2 tsp snipped chives
salt and black pepper

Poaching is a great way of cooking fish. It keeps it moist, full of flavour and low in calories.

STEP ONE Melt the butter in a medium, lidded frying pan, add the onion and sauté gently over a medium heat for 4–5 minutes. Add the potatoes to the pan and sauté for a further 5 minutes, then add the garlic.

STEP TWO Place the wine in a jug, mix in the flour until smooth then add the stock and thyme.

STEP THREE Add the mixture to the pan, stir, cover, bring to the boil and simmer for 10–12 minutes, or until the potatoes are tender and the sauce has reduced by half.

STEP FOUR Add the sea bream fillets to the pan, skin side up, and scatter over the chopped tomato. Cover again and simmer gently for 5 minutes, or until the fish is cooked. Sprinkle with snipped chives, season and serve.

Makes 6 portions

BEEF WELLINGTON

PREP: 1 HOUR
COOK: 50 MINS,
PLUS CHILLING
AND RESTING

1 kg (2¼ lb) piece of beef fillet
350 g (12 oz) packet puff pastry
a little plain flour, for dusting
1 egg, beaten

FOR THE MUSHROOM
DUXELLES

2 tbsp olive oil, plus extra
    for frying the beef
2 large banana shallots,
    finely chopped
500 g (1 lb 2 oz) chestnut
    mushrooms, finely chopped
1 garlic clove, crushed
1 tbsp chopped fresh
    thyme leaves
50 g (2 oz) fresh white
    breadcrumbs
1 egg, beaten, for brushing
salt and black pepper

Beef Wellington is a real show-stopper for a special occasion and, broken down into simple steps, it's really quite easy to make. I like to use a tasty mushroom duxelles rather than paté, as the layer between the beef and the pastry.

STEP ONE Heat the olive oil for the mushroom duxelles in a frying pan over a high heat. Add the shallots and sauté until soft, then add the mushrooms and garlic and sauté for 5 minutes until any liquid has evaporated. Transfer the mixture to a bowl and leave to cool, then stir in the thyme, breadcrumbs and egg. Season generously.

STEP TWO Heat a little oil in the frying pan over a very high heat. Season the beef then sear it briefly on all sides. Leave to cool, then wrap in clingfilm and chill in the fridge for 30 minutes.

STEP THREE Preheat the oven to 220°C/425°F/Gas 7.

STEP FOUR Roll out the pastry on a lightly floured piece of baking paper to a 40 cm (15 in) square. Put the mushroom filling over the centre of the pastry. Remove the beef from the fridge, take off the clingfilm and place the meat on top of the filling.

STEP FIVE Brush the edges of the pastry with egg wash, fold the pastry up over the beef, sealing it across the top, and brush the folded edges with egg wash. Fold in the sides of the pastry over the ends of the fillet.

STEP SIX Place the Wellington on a baking tray seam side down, so that the seal is underneath. Brush with more egg wash, and decorate with any pastry trimmings. Bake for 35 minutes, until golden brown. Remove from the oven and leave to rest for 15 minutes before slicing.

SEABASS WITH CHERRY TOMATOES, SWEET PEPPERS AND BASIL

PREP: 15 MINS
COOK: 50–55 MINS

350 g (12 oz) baby new
    potatoes, halved
2 peppers, deseeded and
    cut into large chunks
1 red onion, sliced
1 garlic clove, thinly sliced
3 tbsp olive oil
150 ml (¼ pint) chicken stock
12 cherry tomatoes, halved
4 seabass fillets (skin on)
2 tbsp chopped fresh
    basil leaves
1 tbsp balsamic vinegar
salt and black pepper

Preserve the delicate flavour of seabass with this oven-baked recipe. Simply serve with the baby new potatoes and some steamed vegetables.

STEP ONE Preheat the oven to 220°C/425°F/Gas 7 and parboil the halved potatoes for 10 minutes.

STEP TWO Put the parboiled potatoes, peppers, onion and garlic in a shallow roasting tin. Add the olive oil, toss and season well. Roast for 30–35 minutes, until golden and just cooked.

STEP THREE Add the stock to the tin and gently stir the vegetables. Add the tomatoes, then lay the fish skin-side up on top of the vegetables. Return to the oven for a further 10 minutes, or until the fish is cooked through.

STEP FOUR Scatter the basil over the fish and vegetables, and drizzle with the balsamic vinegar before serving.

> **TIP**
> Preheat your baking tin when roasting vegetables in the oven. It takes very little extra effort, but you will get better results.

Makes 4 portions

MISO TUNA WITH EDAMAME

**PREP: 10 MINS, PLUS MARINATING
COOK: 6 MINS**

2 tbsp miso paste
2 tbsp balsamic vinegar
2 tbsp sesame oil
4 x 150 g (5 oz) tuna steaks
2 tbsp sunflower oil
salt and black pepper

FOR THE SALAD
150 g (5 oz) bean sprouts
1 tsp sesame oil
150 g (5 oz) podded
   edamame beans
1 bunch spring onions, sliced
½ red chilli, deseeded
   and thinly sliced

FOR THE DRESSING
1 tbsp sweet chilli sauce
1 tbsp rice wine vinegar
1 tbsp sesame oil

Miso paste, made from fermented soy beans, rice and sometimes barley, can be found in the speciality sections of many supermarkets. It gives fish dishes, salads, dressings and marinades a great depth of flavour.

STEP ONE Combine the miso, balsamic vinegar and sesame oil in a shallow dish. Add the tuna steaks and coat them in the mixture. Cover and leave to marinate for 10 minutes.

STEP TWO Meanwhile, make the salad. Fry the bean sprouts briefly in a little sesame oil, then mix with the remaining salad ingredients in a bowl. Mix the dressing ingredients together, then pour the dressing over the salad. Season well.

STEP THREE Heat the sunflower oil a frying pan until very hot. Remove the tuna steaks from the marinade and fry for about 1½ minutes on each side.

STEP FOUR Spoon a pile of salad onto each plate, and serve the sliced tuna on top.

LINGUINE WITH CLAMS

PREP: 30 MINS, PLUS SOAKING
COOK: 10-15 MINS

500 g (1 lb 2 oz) fresh clams
250 g (9 oz) linguine
2 tbsp olive oil
1 onion, chopped
2 garlic cloves, crushed
½ red chilli, deseeded
  and diced
1 tbsp chopped fresh
  thyme leaves
100 ml (3½ fl oz) white wine
4 tomatoes, skinned (see page
  118), deseeded and chopped
juice of ½ lemon
2 tbsp chopped fresh
  parsley leaves
salt and black pepper
50 g (2 oz) Parmesan cheese,
  grated, to serve (optional)

This is the most delicious seafood pasta recipe, and it is so quick and easy to make. If you haven't cooked clams before it's really simple – try it.

STEP ONE When you buy the clams, rinse them and pop in a large bowl. Discard any clams that are open, or have chipped or broken shells. Just before cooking, soak the clams for 20 minutes in cold water. After 20 minutes, remove the clams with a slotted spoon. Using a firm brush, scrub off any remaining sand or barnacles.

STEP TWO Cook the linguine in a large saucepan of lightly salted boiling water according to the packet instructions. Drain.

STEP THREE Meanwhile, heat the oil in a deep, lidded frying pan over a medium heat. Add the onion, garlic, chilli and thyme and sauté for 3–4 minutes until soft. Add the drained clams and coat them in the oil, then add the wine and chopped tomatoes. Cover and simmer for 3–4 minutes, until all of the clams have opened. Add the cooked linguine to the sauce with the lemon and parsley. Toss together, remove from the heat, season and sprinkle over the Parmesan cheese (if using).

TIP
After you drain pasta, and while it's still hot, grate some Parmesan cheese on top before tossing with the sauce. This helps the sauce stick to the pasta.

Makes 4–6 portions

SALMON AND PRAWN RISOTTO

PREP: 25 MINS
COOK: 30 MINS

a knob of butter
2 thin leeks, trimmed
   and sliced
1 garlic clove, crushed
250 g (9 oz) risotto rice
150 ml (¼ pint) white wine
750 ml (1¼ pints) hot
   fish stock
200 g (7 oz) salmon fillet,
   skinned and cut into
   small cubes
200 g (7 oz) button
   mushrooms, sliced
200 g (7 oz) small, cooked
   prawns
2 tbsp double cream
50 g (2 oz) Parmesan
   cheese, grated
squeeze of lemon juice
3 tbsp snipped chives
salt and black pepper

If you love seafood, you'll love this risotto. It keeps the prawns and salmon tender and juicy, and the hot fish stock and white wine really boost the flavour.

STEP ONE Melt the butter in a large saucepan over a medium heat. Add the leeks and sauté for 5 minutes, then add the garlic, followed by the rice. Pour in the wine and stir until absorbed, then add the hot fish stock, a ladleful at a time, until all of the liquid has been absorbed.

STEP TWO Just before the rice is tender (this will take about 20 minutes), and when all of the stock has been incorporated, add the salmon, mushrooms and prawns.

STEP THREE Simmer gently until the fish is cooked through and the mushrooms have softened.

STEP FOUR Add the double cream, Parmesan cheese, lemon juice and chives, season to taste and stir.

Makes 8 portions

ROASTED VEGETABLE GALETTE

PREP: 30 MINS
COOK: 50 MINS

1 aubergine, cubed

1 red pepper, deseeded
    and diced

2 red onions, peeled and
    sliced into thin wedges

3 tbsp olive oil

3 small courgettes,
    halved lengthways then
    sliced into crescent shapes

375 g (13 oz) packet ready-
    rolled puff pastry

a little plain flour, for dusting

1 egg, beaten, for brushing

3 tbsp sundried tomato paste

1 tbsp chopped fresh
    thyme leaves

2 x 240 g (9 oz) packets
    mozzarella cheese, sliced

75 g (3 oz) Cheddar
    cheese, grated

salt and black pepper

Using ready-rolled puff pastry as a base for this delicious galette turns it into a super-easy dish. Try this alternative, too: spread the pastry with pesto and top with ham, sliced tomatoes and fresh basil, sprinkling over grated Cheddar and mozzarella before baking.

STEP ONE Preheat the oven to 200°C/400°F/Gas 6, and put a baking sheet in the oven.

STEP TWO Put the aubergine, red pepper and onions on a baking tray. Toss with the olive oil and season to taste. Roast for about 20 minutes, until lightly golden brown. Add the courgettes, then roast for a further 10 minutes. Remove from the oven and set aside to cool.

STEP THREE Roll out the pastry on a lightly floured work surface to a rectangle roughly 35 x 28 cm (14 x 11 in). Score a 2 cm (¾ in) border around the edge with a knife. Pierce the centre of the pastry several times with a fork and brush with a little of the egg wash. Place on the preheated baking sheet and bake for 10–12 minutes. Remove from the oven, press down the centre within the scored line, spread with the sundried tomato paste and sprinkle with fresh thyme. Arrange the cooled roasted vegetables on top. Season, arrange the mozzarella slices on top of the vegetables and sprinkle over the Cheddar. Brush the border of the pastry with a little more beaten egg.

STEP FOUR Bake for about 10 minutes, or until browned on top and golden and crisp underneath. Remove from the oven, slice into 8 rectangles and serve.

Chapter seven
SWEETS

MANGO, APPLE AND OAT BARS

**PREP: 15 MINS,
PLUS CHILLING
COOK: 3 MINS**

75 g (3 oz) unsalted butter
50 g (2 oz) golden syrup
50 g (2 oz) demerara sugar
50 g (2 oz) soft dried apple,
    roughly chopped
50 g (2 oz) soft dried mango,
    roughly chopped
30 g (1¼ oz) dried cranberries,
    roughly chopped
100 g (4 oz) porridge oats
25 g (1 oz) Rice Krispies
20 g (¾ oz) desiccated coconut

These nutritious bars are great for boosting energy levels, and make a perfect on-the-go snack.

STEP ONE Line a 20 cm (8 in) square baking tin with non-stick baking paper.

STEP TWO Put the butter, golden syrup and sugar in a saucepan and heat until melted. Add the remaining ingredients and mix until combined.

STEP THREE Spoon into the prepared tin. Cover with clingfilm, then press down with your hands to flatten the mixture and level the top. Chill in the fridge for 1 hour, then remove the clingfilm and cut into 8 bars.

TIP
Vary the fruit, substituting with other dried fruits like apricots or raisins. Seeds work well too, giving the bars a nutritional boost: try adding 50 g (2 oz) of sesame, sunflower or pumpkin seeds with the other ingredients in step two.

GOLDEN SYRUP GINGER CAKE

PREP: 12 MINS
COOK: 1–1½ HOURS

125 g (4½ oz) self-raising flour
100 g (4 oz) caster sugar
1 tsp ground cinnamon
¾ tsp ground ginger
2 large eggs, lightly beaten
75 ml (3 fl oz) sunflower oil,
    plus extra for greasing
150 g (5 oz) golden syrup

This deliciously moist, gently spiced cake is perfect for an afternoon tea treat.

STEP ONE Preheat the oven to 150°C/300°F/Gas 2, then line the base of a 900 g (2 lb) loaf tin with non-stick baking paper and grease the sides.

STEP TWO Combine the dry ingredients in a bowl. Mix together the wet ingredients, along with 100 ml (3½ fl oz) water, then add them to the dry ingredients. Beat well, then pour the batter into the prepared tin.

STEP THREE Bake for 1–1½ hours, until the centre is well risen and firm. Leave to cool a little in the tin, then transfer to a wire rack to cool down fully. Cut into slices to serve.

BERRY AND WHITE CHOC TART

PREP: 25 MINS, PLUS CHILLING

125 g (4½ oz) unsalted butter
250 g (9 oz) digestive biscuits
275 g (10 oz) full-fat
   cream cheese
300 ml (½ pint) double cream
100 g (4 oz) white chocolate
2 tbsp maple syrup
1 tsp vanilla extract
300 g (11 oz) fresh blueberries
300 g (11 oz) fresh raspberries
runny honey, for drizzling

This show-stopping dessert couldn't be simpler. The buttery biscuit base is covered with a delicious combination of cream cheese and smooth white chocolate, then topped with fresh berries, which you could swap for whichever fruits are in season.

STEP ONE Start by making the biscuit base. Melt the butter in a saucepan then remove from the heat. Put the biscuits in a plastic food bag, seal the bag, then crush them to fine crumbs with a rolling pin. Transfer the biscuit crumbs to the pan with the melted butter and mix thoroughly. Press the buttery crumbs into the base and slightly up the sides of a 25 cm (10 in) fluted, loose-bottom tart tin. Chill in the fridge for 30 minutes, until firm.

STEP TWO Melt half the white chocolate in a heatproof bowl over a pan of gently simmering water (don't allow the base of the bowl to touch the water), then set aside.

STEP THREE Place the cream cheese and double cream in a bowl. Beat with an electric whisk or by hand until the mixture forms thick, soft peaks, then add the melted white chocolate, maple syrup and vanilla extract. Stir until smooth.

STEP FOUR Remove the biscuit base from the fridge and spoon the cream cheese mixture onto the base. Smooth the surface, arrange the blueberries and raspberries on top, then decorate the tart with white chocolate shavings (using the remaining white chocolate) and drizzle with honey.

INDIVIDUAL STRAWBERRY CHEESECAKES

PREP: 15 MINS

150 ml (¼ pint) double cream
275 g (10 oz) full-fat
   cream cheese
4–5 tbsp maple syrup
   (to taste), plus extra
   for drizzling
350 g (12 oz) fresh
   strawberries, hulled
8 digestive biscuits, crushed
   (see page 184)

You can make these delicious individual puddings in a matter of minutes. Try substituting a little Greek yogurt for the double cream if you like, but not too much, as you'll lose the pretty layers.

STEP ONE Whisk the double cream until it forms soft peaks. Place the cream cheese in a mixing bowl and whisk to loosen, then fold in the whisked cream and maple syrup.

STEP TWO Blend 200 g (7 oz) of the strawberries in the bowl of a food processor until smooth, add to the cream mixture and fold through. Chop the remaining strawberries.

STEP THREE Divide the crushed biscuits between 4 glasses, reserving a few crumbs for the topping. Put two-thirds of the strawberry cream mixture on top. Arrange the chopped strawberries on top of the cream, then spoon the remaining third of the strawberry cream mixture on top.

STEP FOUR Sprinkle the remaining biscuit crumbs over the top and garnish with a sliced strawberry. Chill in the fridge until ready to serve, then drizzle with a little more syrup.

PEACHES, MARSALA AND MASCARPONE

PREP: 15 MINS

250 g (9 oz) mascarpone
6 tbsp Marsala wine,
    plus extra for drizzling
6 tbsp icing sugar, sifted
300 ml (½ pint) double cream
2 large, ripe peaches, peeled,
    stoned and finely diced
75 g (3 oz) amaretti biscuits,
    roughly crushed, plus
    extra to serve

A fantastic, simple yet elegant summer dessert that tastes great with its fresh, ripe peaches.

STEP ONE Put the mascarpone in a bowl. Beat it with an electric whisk or by hand until smooth. Add the Marsala, icing sugar and double cream. Whisk again until the cream forms thick, soft peaks.

STEP TWO Divide half of the diced peaches between 6 wine glasses. Drizzle over a little more Marsala. Divide half of the cream mixture between the 6 glasses, followed by half of the amaretti biscuits. Add the remaining diced peaches, cream and amaretti. Cover and chill in the fridge until ready to serve. Add roughly broken amaretti to decorate.

Makes 8 portions

RASPBERRY CHOCOLATE CAKE

PREP: 20 MINS
COOK: 30–35 MINS

25 g (1 oz) cocoa powder
150 g (5 oz) caster sugar
3 medium eggs, lightly beaten
175 g (6 oz) self-raising flour
1 tsp bicarbonate of soda
1 tsp baking powder
2 tbsp golden syrup
100 ml (3½ fl oz) whole milk
150 ml (¼ pint) sunflower oil,
    plus extra for greasing
fresh raspberries and cherries,
    to decorate
dark chocolate shavings,
    to decorate (optional)

FOR THE ICING
AND FILLING
1½ tbsp cocoa powder, sifted
100 g (4 oz) dark chocolate
    (70% cocoa solids), broken
    into small pieces
150 g (5 oz) unsalted butter,
    softened
375 g (13 oz) icing sugar, sifted
½ tsp vanilla extract
a pinch of salt
1–2 tbsp whole milk (optional)
600 ml (1 pint) double cream
4–5 tbsp raspberry jam

The raspberries give this rich chocolate cake a welcome fruity boost, and using sunflower oil instead of butter gives it a light, moist texture.

STEP ONE Preheat the oven to 160°C/325°F/Gas 3 then grease and line the base of two 20 cm (8 in) round cake tins.

STEP TWO Place all of the ingredients for the cake in a large bowl. Beat until smooth using an electric whisk. Spoon the cake batter into the prepared tins, level the tops and bake for 30–35 minutes, until well risen and coming away from the sides of the tin. Remove from the tins and transfer to a wire rack to cool down completely.

STEP THREE To make the icing, mix the cocoa powder with 3 tablespoons of boiling water and set aside. Melt the chocolate in a heatproof bowl over a pan of gently simmering water (don't allow the base of the bowl to touch the water), then set aside. Beat the butter, icing sugar, vanilla extract and salt together in a large bowl until smooth, using an electric whisk, then add the melted chocolate and cocoa mixture. Beat for a few minutes until thick and creamy, adding a little milk to thin it out if necessary.

STEP FOUR Whisk the double cream until it holds soft peaks, then sandwich the cooled cakes together with the raspberry jam and cream. Spread the icing on top of the cake. Decorate with fresh raspberries and cherries, and shavings of dark chocolate (if you like).

TIP
Run your knife under hot water before cutting the cake, to get perfect, clean slices.

Makes 25 squares

ROCKY ROAD

PREP: 12 MINS, PLUS CHILLING

400 g (14 oz) dark chocolate (70% cocoa solids), broken into small pieces
100 g (4 oz) unsalted butter
100 ml (3½ fl oz) double cream
200 g (7 oz) digestive biscuits, broken into pieces
100 g (4 oz) mini marshmallows
4 x 28 g (1 oz) Crunchie bars, broken into pieces

Who doesn't love a classic Rocky Road refrigerator cake, made with mini pink and white marshmallows, chunks of digestive biscuit and my 'secret' ingredient – a Crunchie bar. It's an easy one to make with the kids: they love it, and once you try it you will find you're hiding pieces away for yourself!

STEP ONE Line a shallow 20 cm (8 in) square baking tin with clingfilm.

STEP TWO Melt the chocolate and butter with the double cream in a heatproof bowl over a pan of gently simmering water (don't allow the base of the bowl to touch the water), then stir, set aside and leave to cool.

STEP THREE Add the remaining ingredients to the melted chocolate mixture and mix well. Spoon into the prepared tin, press down to level the mixture and chill for 2 hours, or until set. Cut into squares and store in the fridge.

*Makes 20 cookies
(freezer friendly
– baked)*

APRICOT, PECAN, RAISIN AND CHOCOLATE COOKIES

**PREP: 20 MINS
COOK: 10–12 MINS**

100 g (4 oz) unsalted
butter, softened
100 g (4 oz) light soft
brown sugar
1 large egg
150 g (5 oz) porridge oats
75 g (3 oz) self-raising
flour, sifted
a pinch of salt
1 tsp vanilla extract
50 g (2 oz) dried apricots,
roughly chopped
50 g (2 oz) raisins
25 g (1 oz) pecans,
roughly chopped
100 g (4 oz) dark chocolate
chips or chopped dark
chocolate (70% cocoa solids)

I've developed many cookie recipes, but none as delicious as this one. You pretty much can't go wrong. If you like, swap plain dark chocolate for sea salt-spiked dark chocolate – it works really well.

STEP ONE Preheat the oven to 180°C/350°F/Gas 4 and line two large baking sheets with non-stick baking paper.

STEP TWO Cream the butter with the sugar in a bowl until light and fluffy, then add the egg and beat again. Fold in the remaining ingredients until well incorporated.

STEP THREE Shape the cookie dough into 20 balls. Place on the prepared baking sheets, well spaced apart, and press down slightly to flatten. Bake for 10–12 minutes, until lightly golden but still slightly soft in the middle. Leave to cool on the sheets for a few minutes, then transfer to a wire rack to cool completely.

TIP
To keep brown sugar soft,
pop a couple of marshmallows
in the bag and seal.

APPLE MUFFINS WITH CINNAMON AND GINGER TOPPING

PREP: 18 MINS
COOK: 20 MINS

250 g (9 oz) self-raising flour
2 tsp ground cinnamon
2 tsp ground ginger
2 tsp baking powder
75 g (3 oz) dark soft
   brown sugar
2 large eggs, lightly beaten
100 ml (3½ fl oz) sunflower oil
8 tbsp whole milk
2 tsp vanilla extract
2 dessert apples, peeled
   and grated
75 g (3 oz) raisins

FOR THE TOPPING
3 tbsp dark soft brown sugar
1 tsp ground cinnamon
1 tsp ground ginger
runny honey, for drizzling
   (optional)

These cinnamon-apple muffins are great served warm. They're also perfect for pudding or breakfast, and keep well for a few days in an airtight container.

STEP ONE Preheat the oven to 180°C/350°F/Gas 4 and line a 12-hole muffin tray with paper cases.

STEP TWO Sift the flour, spices and baking powder into a large mixing bowl and add the sugar.

STEP THREE In a separate bowl, combine the eggs, sunflower oil, milk and vanilla extract. Whisk lightly until blended, then fold the wet ingredients into the dry ones. Add the grated apple and raisins, then gently mix until just combined. Divide evenly between the paper cases.

STEP FOUR Mix together the topping ingredients and sprinkle the topping over the muffin batter in the cases.

STEP FIVE Bake for 20 minutes, until well risen and golden brown. Remove from the oven, leave in the tray for a few minutes, then transfer the muffins to a wire rack and leave to cool. Drizzle with a little honey to serve, if you like.

Makes 8 portions

PLUM AND ALMOND CAKE

PREP: 20 MINS
COOK: 1¼–1½ HOURS

175 g (6 oz) unsalted butter,
   softened
175 g (6 oz) caster sugar
3 large eggs, separated
125 g (4½ oz) ground almonds
1 tsp almond extract
1 tsp baking powder
50 g (2 oz) self-raising flour
4 large, ripe plums, stoned
   and thinly sliced
3 tbsp demerara sugar
icing sugar, for dusting

Serve up a slice of this moist plum and almond cake with a dash of cream. It's the perfect afternoon pick-me-up.

STEP ONE Preheat the oven to 160°C/325°F/Gas 3 then grease and line the base of a 20 cm (8 in) round springform cake tin.

STEP TWO Beat the butter and sugar in a mixing bowl until light and fluffy, then whisk in the egg yolks. Fold in the ground almonds, almond extract, baking powder and flour.

STEP THREE Whisk the eggs whites in a spotlessly clean, grease-free bowl until stiff, then fold them gently into the cake mixture. Fold half of the sliced plums into the mixture and spoon it into the prepared tin, levelling the surface.

STEP FOUR Arrange the remaining sliced plums on the top of the cake mixture and sprinkle with the demerara sugar. Bake for 1¼–1½ hours, until lightly golden and shrinking away from the sides of the tin. Leave to cool in the tin, then remove from the tin and dust with icing sugar to serve.

TIP
If you need to soften butter in a hurry, place it in a sealable plastic bag and leave it into a bowl of warm water for about 4 minutes.

Makes 6–8 portions

CHOCOLATE AND PEAR PUDDING

PREP: 12 MINS
COOK: 20–25 MINS

75 g (3 oz) self-raising flour
25 g (1 oz) cocoa powder
1 tsp baking powder
75 g (3 oz) unsalted butter,
    softened
75 g (3 oz) caster sugar
2 large eggs, lightly beaten
200 g (7 oz) dark chocolate
    (70% cocoa solids)
4 x 415 g (14½ oz) cans
    pear halves in natural
    juice, drained
150 ml (¼ pint) double cream

This hot, gooey chocolate pudding mixed with juicy canned pears is so simple to put together. For the best results, make sure that your butter and eggs are at room temperature.

STEP ONE Preheat the oven to 180°C/350°F/Gas 4 and line the base of a 23 cm (9 in) round springform cake tin with non-stick baking paper.

STEP TWO Sift the flour, cocoa powder and baking powder into a bowl, add the butter, caster sugar and eggs and mix. Melt 50 g (2 oz) of the chocolate in a heatproof bowl over a pan of gently simmering water (don't allow the base of the bowl to touch the water). Add the melted chocolate to the batter. Beat until combined, then spread the batter evenly over the base of the prepared tin.

STEP THREE Slice each pear half into half again lengthways. Arrange the pieces of pear on top of the chocolate sponge batter. Bake for 20–25 minutes until the sponge is well risen and shrinking from the sides of the tin. Leave the sponge to cool in the tin.

STEP FOUR Melt the remaining chocolate with the cream in a heatproof bowl over a pan of simmering water, then drizzle a few tablespoons of the sauce over the pudding, serving the rest alongside.

Makes 20 cookies (freezer friendly – unbaked)

CHOCOLATE AND OAT COOKIES

PREP: 25 MINS
COOK: 15–18 MINS

125 g (4½ oz) unsalted
   butter, softened
150 g (5 oz) light soft
   brown sugar
1 large egg
1½ tsp vanilla extract
a pinch of salt
1 tsp ground ginger
140 g (4¾ oz) plain flour
½ tsp baking powder
75 g (3 oz) porridge oats
150 g (5 oz) dark chocolate
   (70% cocoa solids), chopped,
   or chocolate chips

These sweet oat cookies are great for slow energy release throughout the day.

STEP ONE Preheat the oven to 160°C/325°F/Gas 3 and line two baking sheets with non-stick baking paper.

STEP TWO Cream the softened butter with the sugar in a bowl until light and fluffy. Whisk in the egg and vanilla extract, then fold in the remaining ingredients until combined.

STEP THREE Shape the cookie dough into 20 balls. Place the balls of cookie dough on the prepared baking sheets, spaced apart, and press down slightly to flatten. Bake for 15–18 minutes, until lightly golden. Leave to cool on the sheets for a few minutes, then transfer to a wire rack to cool completely.

TIP
If you want fresh cookies, but don't want to bake a whole batch, split the dough in half. Whilst one half is baking, take the leftover dough and form into balls and arrange them on a baking tray lined with non-stick baking paper. Freeze, then put the unbaked cookies in a plastic bag or airtight plastic container and store in the freezer, ready to bake from frozen.

Makes 8 portions

DARK CHOCOLATE AND GINGER TORTE

PREP: 15 MINS, PLUS CHILLING AND FREEZING

250 g (9 oz) dark chocolate (70% cocoa solids), broken into small pieces
2 tbsp golden syrup
600 ml (1 pint) double cream
1 tbsp instant coffee granules, dissolved in 1 tbsp boiling water

TO DECORATE
75 g (3 oz) ginger biscuits, finely crushed (see page 184)
50 g (2 oz) dark chocolate, chopped

This torte is a chocoholic's dream. Put a little zest into your pud with crushed ginger biscuits.

STEP ONE Melt the chocolate with the golden syrup and 150 ml (¼ pint) of the double cream in a heatproof bowl over a pan of gently simmering water (don't allow the base of the bowl to touch the water), then stir, set aside and leave to cool.

STEP TWO Dampen the inside of a 20 cm (8 in) round springform cake tin, and line the base and sides with clingfilm.

STEP THREE Whip the remaining double cream in a large bowl until soft peaks form. Fold 2 tablespoons of the whipped cream into the melted chocolate mixture, then fold the chocolate mixture into the whipped cream with the coffee. Fold gently until the mixture is smooth and evenly mixed.

STEP FOUR Spoon the mixture into the prepared tin and level the surface. Chill in the fridge for 1 hour, or until firm. Before serving, transfer the torte to the freezer for 15 minutes, then turn it upside down onto a serving plate. Remove the clingfilm and sprinkle over the crushed ginger biscuits. Decorate with chopped chocolate to serve.

APPLE PUDDING

PREP: 20 MINS
COOK: 30 MINS

500 g (1 lb 2 oz) Bramley
   apples, peeled, cored
   and thickly sliced
200 g (7 oz) caster sugar
2 large eggs, lightly beaten
100 g (4 oz) unsalted
   butter, softened
75 g (3 oz) self-raising
   flour, sifted
25 g (1 oz) ground almonds
½ tsp almond extract

Use Bramley apples for this pudding, and serve it on its own or with cream, custard or ice-cream. Everyone will be back for seconds.

STEP ONE Preheat the oven to 180°C/350°F/Gas 4 and grease a 900 ml–1.2 litre (1½ –2 pint) shallow, rectangular ovenproof dish.

STEP TWO Arrange the apples in the base of the dish and sprinkle with half of the caster sugar.

STEP THREE Whisk all the remaining ingredients together in a bowl until smooth. Spread the batter over the top of the apples and bake for 30 minutes, until golden and well risen.

MINI TROPICAL PAVLOVAS

PREP: 20 MINS
COOK: 40–45 MINS,
PLUS COOLING

3 large egg whites, at
    room temperature
175 g (6 oz) caster sugar
200 ml (7 fl oz) double cream
200 g (7 oz) natural
    Greek yogurt
1 ripe mango, peeled,
    stoned and sliced
150 g (5 oz) fresh redcurrants
2 passion fruit

Go tropical with your pavlovas by using fresh mango and passion fruit.

STEP ONE Preheat the oven to 150°C/300°F/Gas 2 and line 2 baking sheets with non-stick baking paper.

STEP TWO Whisk the egg whites in a large, spotlessly clean mixing bowl until they form stiff peaks, then whisk in the caster sugar, a teaspoon at a time, until the mixture is stiff and glossy.

STEP THREE Spoon large tablespoons of the meringue mixture onto the prepared baking sheets to make 6–8 mini pavlovas. Using a teaspoon, spread each meringue out into a rough circle and make a dip in the centre.

STEP FOUR Put the meringues in the oven, then turn down the temperature to 130°C/250°F/Gas ½ and bake for 40–45 minutes until firm to the touch and lightly golden in colour. Turn off the oven, leaving the meringues inside and the oven door closed, so that they cool slowly for another hour. Remove from the oven and remove from the baking sheets.

STEP FIVE Whisk the double cream until it forms stiff peaks, then fold in the Greek yogurt. Divide the mixture between each pavlova, then arrange the mango and redcurrants on top. Slice the passion fruit in half, scoop out the seeds and pulp and scatter over the top of each meringue.

Makes 6 jellies

RASPBERRY AND PROSECCO JELLIES

PREP: 15 MINS,
PLUS CHILLING
COOK: 10 MINS

400 g (14 oz) fresh raspberries,
    plus extra to serve
200 g (7 oz) caster sugar
7 leaves gelatine
600 ml (1 pint) Prosecco or
    Cava (omit for children)

A delicious, light summer treat. Sit back in the sunshine and eat these jellies, spiked with alcohol if you like, with fresh raspberries on the inside.

STEP ONE Place 300 g (11 oz) of the raspberries in a saucepan over a low heat. Add the sugar and 150 ml (¼ pint) water. Cook gently until the sugar has dissolved, then bring to the boil. Simmer for a few minutes until the raspberries have broken down.

STEP TWO Meanwhile, place the gelatine leaves in a bowl of cold water and leave to soak for 5 minutes.

STEP THREE Push the raspberry purée through a sieve into a bowl. Leave to cool slightly, then add the gelatine leaves and stir until dissolved.

STEP FOUR Add the Prosecco or Cava, if using, and stir. Pour into a jug then half-fill 6 wine glasses. Top each serving with the reserved raspberries and chill in the fridge for 2–3 hours, or until set. When they are firm, pour the remaining jelly on top of the raspberries in each glass and chill again until completely set. Serve with extra raspberries on top.

Makes 12 muffins (freezer friendly – without the icing)

MY FAVOURITE CHOCOLATE MUFFINS

PREP: 20 MINS
COOK: 20–25 MINS

100 g (4 oz) dark chocolate (70% cocoa solids), broken into pieces, plus an extra 50 g (2 oz) to decorate
175 g (6 oz) unsalted butter
225 g (8 oz) caster sugar
3 large eggs, at room temperature
225 g (8 oz) self-raising flour
20 g (¾ oz) cocoa powder
a pinch of salt

FOR THE CHOCOLATE BUTTERCREAM ICING
70 g (2½ oz) unsalted butter, softened
150 g (5 oz) icing sugar, sifted
2 tbsp cocoa powder
1 tbsp milk

My family and I love these chocolate muffins. They are gorgeously rich and tasty, especially with a generous layer of chocolate buttercream icing on top.

STEP ONE Preheat the oven to 160°C/325°F/Gas 3 and line a 12-hole muffin tray with paper cases.

STEP TWO Melt the chocolate and butter together in a heatproof bowl over a pan of gently simmering water (don't allow the base of the bowl to touch the water). Remove from the heat and leave to cool.

STEP THREE Beat the sugar and eggs in a bowl until thick and creamy, then fold into the cooled chocolate mixture. Sift in the flour, cocoa powder and salt and whisk for a further 20 seconds.

STEP FOUR Divide the batter evenly between the paper cases. Bake for 20–25 minutes, until well risen and just firm in the middle. Leave to cool for a few minutes in the muffin tray before transferring to a wire rack to cool completely.

STEP FIVE To make the icing, beat the softened butter with half of the icing sugar until smooth, then add the remaining sugar, cocoa powder and milk. Whisk until fluffy.

STEP SIX Pipe or spread the buttercream icing onto the muffins, then chop or grate the remaining 50 g (2 oz) chocolate to decorate the tops.

Makes 4 portions

BANANA CARAMEL

PREP: 8 MINS
COOK: 6 MINS

75 g (3 oz) unsalted butter

75 g (3 oz) light soft brown
   sugar

4 large, ripe bananas, peeled
   and halved lengthways

2–3 tbsp brandy
   (omit for children)

4 tbsp double cream

This dessert is so simple and easy to make. Watch the bananas caramelise in the buttery caramel and add some brandy for the grown-ups, too.

STEP ONE Melt the butter and sugar in a non-stick frying pan over a medium heat for a couple of minutes until the sugar has dissolved. Add the bananas and fry gently for 2–3 minutes, coating the bananas in the caramel.

STEP TWO Add the brandy, if using, then carefully transfer the bananas to a plate. Add the double cream to the pan, stir over the heat, then drizzle the sauce over the bananas.

TIP
Speed up ripening by putting fruit into a paper bag. When fruit is kept in the bag, concentrated ethylene gas helps it ripen faster.

INTRODUCTION

A

all'arrabbiata, penne 130
almond
    plum and almond cake
      198–9
    trout with almonds 36–7
apple
    apple muffins with cinnamon
      and ginger topping 196–7
    apple pudding 203
    mango, apple and oat
      bars 182
    roast loin of pork with roast
      potatoes and gravy 88–9
apricot, pecan, raisin and
    chocolate cookies 193–5
aubergine
    aubergine parmigiana 78–9
    roasted vegetable galette
      177–9
avocado
    beef, red pepper and pickled
      red onion wrap 114–15
    chicken, avocado and tomato
      wrap 112

B

bacon
    bacon and pea risotto 46–7
    chicken, bacon and tomato
      lasagne 86
    penne with roasted
      butternut squash and
      bacon 147
baguettes, steak baguettes
    with tomato and onion
    relish 38–9
balsamic chicken with white
    wine 152
banana caramel 210–11
bang bang chicken salad 102
barbeque sauce, chicken in 26

bars
    Cheryl's power seed bars
      108–9
    mango, apple and oat bars
      182
bean(s)
    bean and sausage hotpot 145
    chilli beef casserole 94
beef
    beef, red pepper and pickled
      red onion wrap 114–15
    beef noodle salad 116
    beef with oyster sauce,
      peppers, and broccoli 40–1
    beef in red wine sauce 162
    beef wellington 167–9
    chilli beef casserole 94
    curried beef goulash 96–7
    meatloaf 90
    minced beef croquettes 91
    pasta meatball bake 77
    steak baguettes with tomato
      and onion relish 38–9
berry and white choc tart 184–5
biscuit
    biscuit bases 184–5, 186–7
    rocky road 192
blue cheese
    blue cheese dressing 17
    pappardelle with Dolcelatte,
      spinach and tomato 28–9
    three-cheese rigatoni 45
bolognese, chicken bolognese
    with penne 22
Bran flakes, Cheryl's power
    seed bars 108–9
bread
    falafel-style vegetables bites
      134–5
    spaghetti with tomatoes,
      pesto and ciabatta crumbs
      139
    see also ciabatta bread

breadcrumbs
    beef wellington 167–9
    lamb burgers with salsa
      92–3
    meatloaf 90
    pasta meatball bake 77
    turkey meatloaf meatballs
      95
    see also panko breadcrumbs
broccoli
    beef noodle salad 116
    beef with oyster sauce,
      peppers, and broccoli
      40–1
    mushroom and broccoli
      pasta 44
    stuffed veggie potato 62
    see also Tenderstem broccoli
bruschetta, three-tomato
    118–19
burgers, lamb burgers with
    salsa 92–3
butter parsley 31
buttercream icing, chocolate
    208–9
butternut squash
    chicken and vegetable
      chowder 16
    Moroccan chicken with
      butternut squash and red
      onion couscous 80–1
    penne with roasted
      butternut squash and
      bacon 147

C

cakes
    golden syrup ginger cake 183
    plum and almond cake 198–9
    raspberry chocolate cake
      190–1
caramel, banana 210–11

carrot
  beef noodle salad 116
  carrot and coriander soup
    131
  chicken chow mein 18–19
  crunchy sweetcorn salsa
    salad 104–5
  one-pot chicken with spring
    vegetables 164–5
  salmon and cod gratin 98–9
  sausages with cheesy mash
    and onion gravy 144
  venison casserole 156
casserole
  chilli beef 94
  venison 156
cauliflower, roasted 63–5
Cheddar
  cheese sauce 86
  cheese straws with pesto and
    thyme 122
  chicken, avocado and tomato
    wrap 112
  frittata with cherry tomato
    136–7
  pasta meatball bake 77
  roasted vegetable galette
    177–9
  salmon and cod gratin 98–9
  sausage and bean hotpot 145
  stuffed veggie potato 62
  three-cheese rigatoni 45
cheese
  cheese sauce 86
  cheese straws with pesto and
    thyme 122
  cheesy sauce 32
  mini cheese and tomato
    tartlets 126–7
  three-cheese rigatoni 45
  see also specific cheeses
cheesecakes, individual
    strawberry 186–7
chicken 12
  balsamic chicken with white
    wine 152

bang bang chicken salad 102
chicken, avocado and tomato
  wrap 112
chicken, bacon and tomato
  lasagne 86
chicken in barbeque sauce 26
chicken bolognese with
  penne 22
chicken, cherry tomato and
  mozzarella salad 103
chicken chow mein 18–19
chicken in a creamy
  mushroom sauce 151
chicken goujons wrapped in
  Parma ham 56–7
chicken and vegetable
  chowder 16
chicken and vermicelli Thai
  rice wraps 106–7
fettuccine with chicken and
  spinach 23
honey chicken and hummus
  wrap 113
honey-glazed chicken with
  lemon and thyme 54
Indian-spiced chicken with
  rice 142–3
Italian rice salad 110–11
Mediterranean oven-baked
  chicken drumsticks 82–3
Moroccan chicken with
  butternut squash and red
  onion couscous 80–1
one-pot chicken with spring
  vegetables 164–5
roasted chicken and tarragon
  pappardelle 52–3
sticky coconut chicken thighs
  84–5
stuffed peppers with rice and
  chicken 163
chickpeas, falafel-style
  vegetables bites 134–5
chilli
  chilli beef casserole 94
  garlic and chilli prawns 72–3

Chinese-style rice 157–9
chocolate 12
  apricot, pecan, raisin and
    chocolate cookies 193–5
  chocolate buttercream icing
    208–9
  chocolate and oat
    cookies 201
  chocolate and pear pudding
    200
  dark chocolate and ginger
    torte 202
  my favourite chocolate
    muffins 208–9
  raspberry chocolate cake
    190–1
  rocky road 192
chowder, chicken and
  vegetable 16
ciabatta bread
  chicken, cherry tomato and
    mozzarella salad 103
  spaghetti with tomatoes,
    pesto and ciabatta crumbs
    139
cinnamon and ginger topping
  with apple muffins 196–7
clam with linguini 174–5
coconut chicken thighs,
  sticky 84–5
cod
  cod in cheesy sauce 32
  salmon and cod gratin 98–9
cookies
  apricot, pecan, raisin and
    chocolate 193–5
  chocolate and oat 201
courgette
  courgette `spaghetti' 66–7
  griddled courgettes with
    balsamic glaze 70–1
  roasted vegetable galette
    177–9
couscous, Moroccan chicken
    with butternut squash and
    red onion couscous 80–1

cream cheese
   berry and white choc tart
      184–5
   individual strawberry
      cheesecakes 186–7
crème fraiche 12
   carrot and coriander soup 131
   chicken goujons wrapped
      in Parma ham 56–7
   fettuccine with chicken and
      spinach 23
   mushroom and broccoli
      pasta 44
   prawn in a light curried
      sauce 33
   roasted chicken and tarragon
      pappardelle 52–3
   three-cheese rigatoni 45
croquettes, minced beef 91
Crunchie, rocky road 192
cucumber
   bang bang chicken salad 102
   chicken, cherry tomato and
      mozzarella salad 103
   melon, cucumber and cherry
      tomato salad 124–5
   salsa 68–9, 92–3
   tzatziki 134–5
curry
   curried beef goulash 96–7
   curried potato salad with
      roasted peppers 123
   curried sweetcorn fritters
      68–9
   prawns in a light curried
      sauce 33

D
dahl, red lentil 138
Dolcelatte, spinach and tomato
   with pappardelle 28–9
Dover sole with herb
   butter 31
dressings 63–5, 102–5, 110,
   116, 124–5, 172–3

blue cheese 17
   honey and ginger 140–1
duck
   duck stir-fry with plum sauce
      24–5
   oriental roast duck with
      Chinese-style rice 157–9

E
edamame
   miso tuna with edamame
      172–3
   quinoa and edamame salad
      with honey and ginger
      dressing 140–1
egg
   frittata with cherry tomato
      136–7
   poached eggs with red onion,
      tomato and pepper ragù
      146
   scrambled eggs with tomato
      and onion 48–9

F
falafel-style vegetables
   bites 134–5
fettuccine with chicken
   and spinach 23
fish
   cod in cheesy sauce 32
   Dover sole with herb
      butter 31
   herb-crusted salmon 49–51
   miso tuna with edamame
      172–3
   salmon and cod gratin 98–9
   trout with almonds 36–7
fresh cream desserts
   raspberry chocolate
      cake 190
   mini tropical pavlovas 204–5
frittata with cherry tomato
   136–7

fritters, curried sweetcorn
   68–9
fusilli, sausage ragù 87

G
galette, roasted vegetable
   177–9
garlic and chilli prawns 72–3
ginger
   apple muffins with cinnamon
      and ginger topping 196–7
   dark chocolate and ginger
      torte 202
   golden syrup ginger cake 183
   honey and ginger dressing
      140–1
golden syrup ginger cake 183
goujons, chicken goujons
      wrapped in Parma ham
      56–7
goulash, curried beef 96–7
Grape Nuts, Cheryl's power
      seed bars 108–9
gratin
   salmon and cod gratin 98–9
   wild mushroom gratin 153–5
gravy 88–9, 91
   onion 144
gruyère cheese
   sausages with cheesy mash
      and onion gravy 144
   stuffed peppers with rice
      and chicken 163

H
ham
   linguini with 58
   see also Parma ham
herb-crusted salmon 49–51
honey
   honey chicken and hummus
      wrap 113
   honey and ginger dressing
      140–1

honey-glazed chicken with lemon and thyme 54
hotpot, sausage and bean 145
hummus and honey chicken wrap 113

I

Iceberg lettuce and cherry tomato salad with blue cheese dressing 17
icing, chocolate buttercream 208–9
Indian-spiced chicken with rice 142–3
Italian rice salad 110–11

J

jellies, raspberry and prosecco 206–7

L

lamb
    lamb burgers with salsa 92–3
    slow-roasted shoulder of lamb with potatoes and leeks 160–1
lasagne, chicken, bacon and tomato 86
leek
    salmon and cod gratin 98–9
    slow-roasted shoulder of lamb with potatoes and leeks 160–1
    stuffed veggie potato 62
lentil
    Puy lentil with mushrooms and spinach 20–1
    red lentil dahl 138
    tasty spinach soup 132–3
linguini
    linguini with clams 174–5
    linguini with ham 58

Little Gem lettuce
    bang bang chicken salad 102
    honey chicken and hummus wrap 113

M

mango
    mango, apple and oat bars 182
marshmallow, rocky road 192
mascarpone
    peaches, Marsala and mascarpone 188–9
    tomato and mascarpone sauce 30
meatballs
    pasta meatball bake 77
    turkey meatloaf meatballs 95
meatloaf 90
    turkey meatloaf meatballs 95
melon, cucumber and cherry tomato salad 124–5
meringue, mini tropical pavlovas 204–5
mini tropical pavlovas 204–5
mirin 12
miso tuna with edamame 172–3
Moroccan chicken with butternut squash and red onion couscous 80–1
mozzarella
    aubergine parmigiana 78–9
    chicken, cherry tomato and mozzarella salad 103
    pasta meatball bake 77
    penne with roasted cherry tomatoes and pesto 27
    roasted vegetable galette 177–9
muffins
    apple muffins with cinnamon and ginger topping 196–7
    my favourite chocolate muffins 208–9

mushroom
    beef in red wine sauce 162
    beef wellington 167–9
    chicken bolognese with penne 22
    chicken chow mein 18–19
    chicken in a creamy mushroom sauce 151
    duck stir-fry with plum sauce 24–5
    mushroom and broccoli pasta 44
    oriental roast duck with Chinese-style rice 157–9
    Puy lentil with mushrooms and spinach 20–1
    salmon with prawn risotto 176
    wild mushroom gratin 153–5

N

noodles
    bang bang chicken salad 102
    beef noodle salad 116
    chicken chow mein 18–19
    chicken and vermicelli Thai rice wraps 106–7

O

oat
    apricot, pecan, raisin and chocolate cookies 193–5
    chocolate and oat cookies 201
    mango, apple and oat bars 182
onion
    beef, red pepper and pickled red onion wrap 114–15
    Moroccan chicken with butternut squash and red onion couscous 80–1
    onion gravy 144
    poached eggs with red onion, tomato and pepper ragù 146

roasted vegetable galette
177–9
salsa 68–9
scrambled eggs with tomato
and onion 48–9
tomato and onion relish 38–9
oriental roast duck with
Chinese-style rice 157–9
orzo and prawn confetti salad
120–1
oyster sauce, peppers, and
broccoli with beef 40–1

P
pak choi
chicken chow mein 18–19
duck stir-fry with plum
sauce 24–5
panko breadcrumbs
herb-crusted salmon 49–51
sesame prawn balls 34–5
pappardelle
pappardelle with Dolcelatte,
spinach and tomato 28–9
roasted chicken and tarragon
pappardelle 52–3
Parma ham-wrapped chicken
goujons 56–7
Parmesan 12
aubergine parmigiana 78–9
bacon and pea risotto 46–7
baked tomato risotto 151
cheese straws with pesto and
thyme 122
cheesy sauce 32
chicken, cherry tomato and
mozzarella salad 103
courgette `spaghetti' 66–7
falafel-style vegetables
bites 134–5
fettuccine with chicken
and spinach 23
griddled courgettes with
balsamic glaze 70–1
linguini with clams 174–5

linguini with ham 58
mini cheese and tomato
tartlets 126–7
mushroom and broccoli
pasta 44
pasta meatball bake 77
penne with roasted
butternut squash and
bacon 147
Puy lentil with mushrooms
and spinach 20–1
roasted chicken and tarragon
pappardelle 52–3
salmon and cod gratin 98–9
salmon with prawn risotto 176
sausage ragù 87
spaghetti with tomatoes,
pesto and ciabatta crumbs
139
three-cheese rigatoni 45
wild mushroom gratin 153–5
parsley butter 31
passion fruit, mini tropical
pavlovas 204–5
pasta
chicken, bacon and tomato
lasagne 86
chicken bolognese with
penne 22
fettuccine with chicken and
spinach 23
linguini with clams 174–5
linguini with ham 58
mushroom and broccoli
pasta 44
pappardelle with Dolcelatte,
spinach and tomato 28–9
pasta meatball bake 77
penne all'arrabbiata 130
penne with roasted
butternut squash and
bacon 147
penne with roasted cherry
tomatoes and pesto 27
roasted chicken and tarragon
pappardelle 52–3

sausage ragù 87
spaghetti with tomatoes,
pesto and ciabatta
crumbs 139
three-cheese rigatoni 45
pastry, savoury 126–7
pavlovas, mini tropical
pavlovas 204–5
peach, Marsala and
mascarpone 188–9
pear and chocolate pudding 200
pea(s)
bacon and pea risotto 46–7
Indian-spiced chicken with
rice 142–3
one-pot chicken with spring
vegetables 164–5
oriental roast duck with
Chinese-style rice 157–9
tasty spinach soup 132–3
pecan, raisin, chocolate and
apricot cookies 193–5
penne
chicken bolognese with
penne 22
penne all'arrabbiata 130
penne with roasted
butternut squash and
bacon 147
penne with roasted cherry
tomatoes and pesto 27
pepper
beef, red pepper and pickled
red onion wrap 114–15
beef with oyster sauce,
peppers, and broccoli 40–1
chilli beef casserole 94
crunchy sweetcorn salsa
salad 104–5
curried beef goulash 96–7
curried potato salad with
roasted peppers 123
duck stir-fry with plum
sauce 24–5
Mediterranean oven-baked
chicken drumsticks 82–3

poached eggs with red onion, tomato and pepper ragù 146

roasted vegetable galette 177–9

seabass with cherry tomatoes, sweet peppers and basil 170–1

stuffed peppers with rice and chicken 163

pesto

cheese straws with pesto and thyme 122

chicken goujons wrapped in Parma ham 56–7

courgette 'spaghetti' 66–7

penne with roasted cherry tomatoes and pesto 27

spaghetti with tomatoes, pesto and ciabatta crumbs 139

plum

duck stir-fry with plum sauce 24–5

plum and almond cake 198–9

pork, roast loin of pork with roast potatoes and gravy 88–9

potato

chicken and vegetable chowder 16

curried potato salad with roasted peppers 123

frittata with cherry tomato 136–7

minced beef croquettes 91

one-pot chicken with spring vegetables 164–5

poached sea bream with baby new potatoes 166

roast loin of pork with roast potatoes and gravy 88–9

roasted new potatoes with rosemary 55

salmon and cod gratin 98–9

sausage and bean hotpot 145

sausages with cheesy mash and onion gravy 144

seabass with cherry tomatoes, sweet peppers and basil 170–1

slow-roasted shoulder of lamb with potatoes and leeks 160–1

stuffed veggie potato 62

prawn

garlic and chilli prawns 72–3

orzo and prawn confetti salad 120–1

prawn in a light curried sauce 33

salmon with prawn risotto 176

sesame prawn balls 34–5

spicy prawn wrap 117

prosecco and raspberry jellies 206–7

puff pastry

beef wellington 167–9

cheese straws with pesto and thyme 122

roasted vegetable galette 177–9

Puy lentil with mushrooms and spinach 20–1

Q

quinoa and edamame salad with honey and ginger dressing 140–1

R

ragù

poached eggs with red onion, tomato and pepper ragù 146

sausage ragù 87

raisin, apricot, pecan and chocolate cookies 193–5

raspberry

berry and white choc tart 184–5

raspberry chocolate cake 190–1

raspberry and prosecco jellies 206–7

red wine sauce, beef in 162

redcurrant, mini tropical pavlovas 204–5

relish, tomato and onion 38–9

rice

bacon and pea risotto 46–7

baked tomato risotto 151

Indian-spiced chicken with rice 142–3

Italian rice salad 110–11

oriental roast duck with Chinese-style rice 157–9

salmon with prawn risotto 176

stuffed peppers with rice and chicken 163

rigatoni, three-cheese 45

risotto

bacon and pea risotto 46–7

baked tomato risotto 151

salmon with prawn risotto 176

rocky road 192

roquefort, three-cheese rigatoni 45

S

salads

bang bang chicken salad 102

beef noodle salad 116

chicken, cherry tomato and mozzarella salad 103

crunchy sweetcorn salsa salad 104–5

curried potato salad with roasted peppers 123

Iceberg and cherry tomato salad with blue cheese dressing 17

Italian rice salad 110–11
melon, cucumber and cherry
    tomato salad 124–5
miso tuna with edamame
    172–3
orzo and prawn confetti
    salad 120–1
quinoa and edamame salad
    with honey and ginger
    dressing 140–1
salmon
    herb-crusted salmon 49–51
    salmon and cod gratin 98–9
    salmon with prawn risotto
        176
salsa 68–9, 92–3
    crunchy sweetcorn salsa
        salad 104–5
sausage
    sausage and bean hotpot 145
    sausage ragù 87
    toad in the hole 59
scrambled eggs with tomato
    and onion 48–9
sea bream, poached sea bream
    with baby new potatoes
    166
seabass with cherry tomatoes,
    sweet peppers and basil
    170–1
seed bars, Cheryl's power
    108–9
sesame prawn balls 34–5
shallot 12
sirloin steak
    beef, red pepper and pickled
        red onion wrap 114–15
    beef noodle salad 116
    beef in red wine sauce 162
    steak baguettes with tomato
        and onion relish 38–9
soup
    carrot and coriander
        soup 131
    tasty spinach soup 132–3
`spaghetti', courgette 66–7

spaghetti with tomatoes, pesto
    and ciabatta crumbs 139
spinach
    fettuccine with chicken
        and spinach 23
    pappardelle with Dolcelatte,
        spinach and tomato 28–9
    Puy lentil with mushrooms
        and spinach 20–1
    tasty spinach soup 132–3
spiralizers 10, 60–1, 66
steak
    steak baguettes with tomato
        and onion relish 38–9
    see also sirloin steak
stir-fry, duck stir-fry with
    plum sauce 24–5
strawberry cheesecakes,
    individual 186–7
sugar snap pea(s)
    chicken chow mein 18–19
    duck stir-fry with plum
        sauce 24–5
sweet chilli sauce 12
sweet potato curls 60–1
sweetcorn
    chicken and vegetable
        chowder 16
    crunchy sweetcorn salsa
        salad 104–5
    curried sweetcorn fritters
        68–9
    oriental roast duck with
        Chinese-style rice 157–9
    orzo and prawn confetti
        salad 120–1
    quinoa and edamame salad
        with honey and ginger
        dressing 140–1

T

tarragon pappardelle and
    roasted chicken 52–3
tartlets, mini cheese and
    tomato 126–7

tarts, berry and white choc
    184–5
Tenderstem broccoli, beef
    with oyster sauce, peppers,
    and broccoli 40–1
thyme 12
    cheese straws with pesto
        and thyme 122
toad in the hole 59
tomato 12
    aubergine parmigiana 78–9
    baked tomato risotto 151
    chicken, avocado and tomato
        wrap 112
    chicken, bacon and tomato
        lasagne 86
    chicken bolognese with
        penne 22
    chicken, cherry tomato and
        mozzarella salad 103
    chilled roast tomato soup 76
    chilli beef casserole 94
    courgette `spaghetti' 66–7
    curried beef goulash 96–7
    frittata with cherry tomato
        136–7
    Iceberg and cherry tomato
        salad with blue cheese
        dressing 17
    Indian-spiced chicken with
        rice 142–3
    linguini with clams 174–5
    linguini with ham 58
    Mediterranean oven-baked
        chicken drumsticks 82–3
    melon, cucumber and cherry
        tomato salad 124–5
    mini cheese and tomato
        tartlets 126–7
    Moroccan chicken with
        butternut squash and red
        onion couscous 80–1
    orzo and prawn confetti
        salad 120–1
    pappardelle with Dolcelatte,
        spinach and tomato 28–9

pasta meatball bake 77
penne all'arrabbiata 130
penne with roasted cherry
    tomatoes and pesto 27
poached eggs with red
    onion, tomato and pepper
    ragù 146
red lentil dahl 138
salsa 68–9, 92–3
sausage and bean hotpot 145
sausage ragù 87
scrambled eggs with tomato
    and onion 48–9
seabass with cherry
    tomatoes, sweet peppers
    and basil 170–1
spaghetti with tomatoes,
    pesto and ciabatta
    crumbs 139
stuffed veggie potato 62
three-tomato bruschetta
    118–19
tomato and mascarpone
    sauce 30
tomato and onion relish
    38–9

tomato sauce 90, 163
torte, dark chocolate and
    ginger 202
tropical, mini tropical pavlovas
    204–5
trout with almonds 36–7
tuna, miso tuna with edamame
    172–3
turkey meatloaf meatballs 95
tzatziki 134–5

V
vegetables
    falafel-style vegetables
        bites 134–5
    frozen vegetables 12
    one-pot chicken with spring
        vegetables 164–5
    roasted vegetable galette
        177–9
venison casserole 156
vermicelli and chicken Thai
    rice wraps 106–7

W
white chocolate and berry
    tart 184–5
white wine with balsamic
    chicken 152
wraps
    beef, red pepper and pickled
        red onion 114–15
    chicken, avocado and
        tomato 112
    honey chicken and
        hummus 113
    spicy prawn 117

Y
yogurt
    mini tropical pavlovas 204–5
    tzatziki 134–5
Yorkshire pudding
    batter 59

ANNABEL KARMEL

25 Years of Recipes and Advice

Having spent 25 years devising delicious, wholesome meals
for every age and stage, leading cookery author and food expert
Annabel Karmel MBE is on hand for your food journey.

From pregnancy and weaning through to children's food and family
mealtimes, there are more than 40 books to choose from…